AUTHENTIC ITALIAN COOKING

Welcome From Classico®

When an Italian asks you to *preparata mangiare*—"prepare to eat"—it is more than a summons to enjoy the delectable flavors of a home-cooked meal, it's an invitation to delight in the cook's hospitality, heritage and tradition.

We at Classico invite you to try our authentic sauces and prepare our 100 percent durum semolina Italian pastas. You'll not only savor the delicious, homemade taste Classico is proud of, but you'll indulge in the best authentic regional Italian cuisine.

Classico has taken great care to use favorite regional ingredients in each authentically inspired sauce recipe—from ripe red tomatoes to flavorful vegetables, aromatic cheeses and Italian herbs. So tasting and savoring each Classico sauce is like a visit to an Italian family kitchen—whether it's in Lombardia in the North or Calabria in the South.

Here, between the pages of *Authentic Italian Cooking,* you can experience a culinary tour of Italy and discover the special cooking style of each of its regions. Each recipe, like the ingredients in Classico sauces and pastas, represents the taste preferences and traditions of an individual region. So enjoy your cook's tour of Italy and … *buon appetito!*

CREDITS

Director of Marketing	Kathleen Popp International Gourmet Specialties, Inc.
Product Manager	Debbie Ehrenworth International Gourmet Specialties, Inc.
Recipe Development	Charlene Sneed International Gourmet Specialties, Inc.
Editorial Director	Mary-Ann Lambert Klein & Solin, Inc.
Contributing Food Editor	Shelli McConnell
Associate Design Director	Nancy Wiles Meredith Custom Publishing
Contributing Food Photographers	Andy Lyons, Michael Garland
Contributing Location Photographers	Claudia Dhimitri and Joe Viesti of Viesti Associates, Inc.
Food Stylists	Janet Pittman, Jennifer Peterson, Diana Nolin Meredith Corporation
Contributing Prop Stylist	Carolyn Schultz

Pictured on the cover: Chicken with Summer Vegetables Campania (see recipe, page 71).

CLASSICO®

AUTHENTIC ITALIAN COOKING

Produced by Meredith Custom Publishing, 1912 Grand Ave., Des Moines, IA 50309-3379.

Send correspondence to:
International Gourmet Specialties Company
180 E. Broad St.
Columbus, OH 43215

Authenticity To Savor

If you were to embark on a regional tour of Italy, your taste buds alone would announce your arrival in each new place—for in Italy the delights of the table vary distinctly from region to region. Italians revere the abundant gifts of food that nature has provided their homeland and in each region have created a unique cuisine based on the local vegetables, herbs, seafood and wildlife that have flourished there for centuries. Inspired by this tradition, Classico® invites you to savor an array of recipes reflecting the bountiful ingredients that make up the delicious culinary tapestry called *Authentic Italian Cooking.*

Each recipe is accompanied *Lombardia* by a symbol that denotes its region of origin. To see where a particular dish comes from, find the name on the symbol on this map.

Regions of Italy

A Cook's Tour

FROM THE VERDANT NORTH

Valle d'Aosta, the smallest region of Italy, sits cradled in the northwest corner of the country, bordering France and Switzerland. It is mountainous, and its alpine inclinations show up in its favored foods, such as hearty soups of cabbage, barley and assorted vegetables topped with melted fontina cheese.

The mountains also play a prime role in the food of the **Piemonte** region. The earthy Piemontese like wild game stewed in wine, eaten alongside vegetables such as leeks, bell peppers, garlic, spinach, tomatoes, beets and celery.

Nearly every region of Italy has some form of café society, and Piemonte is no exception. The Piemontese are known to sip hot chocolate in cafés of choice throughout the day.

East of Piemonte is the region of **Lombardia,** which touches the foothills of the Alps and certainly feels their presence. Lombardia's most important

contribution to the cuisine of Italy is cheese. Two of its more famous cheeses include the luxurious, Italian blue cheese, Gorgonzola, and the rich, creamy Bel Paese.

Butter is the favored fat, and cream is used with a generous hand in the dishes of Milan, Lombardia's most influential city.

Trento, the principal city of the mountainous region of **Trentino-Alto Adige,** is renowned for its mushroom market. The Dolomite mountains provide a plethora of mushrooms, including woodsy porcini and buttery chanterelles.

Apples are grown near this region's border with Austria and make their way into local pastries.

The region of **Friuli-Venezia Giulia** also borders Austria—as well as the former Yugoslavia—and the influence of its neighbors is keenly felt. The dishes of Venezia have a distinctively Eastern feel, including the flavorful, paprika-rich *gulasch*.

Only a small bit of the region of **Veneto** touches the Alps, and here the hearty mountain influence finally fades away. Venetians are lovers of refinement and were, in fact, the first Europeans to use a fork—in the 11th century.

Since then, they have been filling their forks with seafood and

7

delicate vegetables grown inland, including *radicchio rosso*—for which the city of Treviso is famous.

The people of **Liguria** live between the sea and mountains that rise up suddenly just a few miles inland. In this land of contrasts they have created a cuisine based on seafood, vegetables, local olive oil, pasta and an array of wild herbs that cling to a rocky coastline, which drops precipitously to the sea.

Pesto, the fragrant sauce made of basil, garlic, Parmesan cheese, olive oil and pine nuts, was born here.

TO THE CULINARY CENTER

The trinity of the table of the **Emilia-Romagna** region is pork,

pasta and Parmesan. It is here that the best prosciutto ham is made, as well as one of the greatest contributions to the world table, Parmesan cheese.

The Emilia-Romagna town of Modena is famous for its world-renowned balsamic vinegar, aged to perfection in special casks.

In **Toscana,** simplicity reigns. Here, the best beef in Italy is raised and Tuscans like it roasted or grilled over an open flame with fresh herbs. Toscana, too, is famous for its hearty soups featuring vegetables, beans, pasta, herbs and olive oil—a staple of the Tuscan table. Typically, a bowl of soup is accompanied with a chunk of crusty, country bread and a glass of its most

famous wine, Chianti.

Connected to Toscana is the region of **Marche,** where the variety of fish is the greatest of anywhere in Italy.

Marche has a beautiful balance of the sea, a rich, fertile countryside and mountains. The Apennine slopes yield white truffles and in the valleys splendid orchards bear apples, peaches and figs.

Umbria, at Italy's center, is blessed with rolling green hills. Black truffles, gathered in the woods, are commonly eaten raw, especially in salads, or stirred into pasta sauces.

The cooking of **Lazio** is the cooking of Rome. Tender pastas and robust sauces play a

prominent role and many dishes are prepared *al arrabbiata,* "in the angry way," with a healthy dose of hot chili peppers.

Directly east of Lazio lie **Abruzzi** and **Molise.** Influenced by both the North, in their fondness for hearty sausages and flavorful cheeses, and the South, in their passion for shaped pastas and fiery chili peppers, these regions straddle Italy's culinary divide.

TO THE SUNNY SOUTH

In **Campania,** the everyday menu is as simple and vibrant as Neapolitan sunshine. Open-air markets abound with tomatoes, vegetables and fresh seafood. Pasta is enjoyed daily and fabulous gelato confections top off an evening stroll.

Gastronomic signs of Greek influence abide in **Puglia,** the

"heel" that points toward Greece. Foods like fava beans, chick peas and octopus, cooked with lemon juice and olive oil, echo their Greek heritage.

As in much of Southern Italy, vegetables, pasta and chili peppers are staples in the region of **Basilicata.**

Calabria, the "toe" of the "boot," is blessed with towering mountains that bear chestnuts and mushrooms. Grapefruit and oranges are also plentiful.

AND TO THE ISLANDS

The scents and colors of the cooking in **Sicilia** often evoke the island's Greek and Arab heritage. Almonds, raisins and fragrant spices frequently appear in the inventively combined dishes Sicilians love, such as *caponata,* a spicy vegetable melange, and in the pasta and seafood dishes that dominate this intriguingly exotic cuisine.

Mediterranean **Sardegna** is Italy's other island region; like Sicilians, Sardegnans maintain a separate identity from mainland Italy in their culture and cuisine.

Sardegnan cooking is both coastal—heavy in fish and lobster—and rustic, reflecting its mountainous interior. Here, meat is cooked with fresh herbs over an open flame and accompanied by pasta—to which cooks often add a pinch of saffron.

And though Sardegna—like all of the regions—maintains a distinct regional pride, its link with Italy is apparent in the Sardegnans' reverence for their windswept island and the gifts of food it provides for their tables.

The North: A Green and Giving Land

From the glacial peaks of Valle d'Aosta to the storybook hill towns of Toscana, Northern Italy is a land of contrasts: breathtaking, snowcapped mountains; green, rolling hills dotted with blue lakes; a rocky, rugged coastline. The land yields an abundance of riches: wild game, grapes, vegetables, fruits, herbs, truffles and seafood. Excellent butter, rich cream and sumptuous cheeses are made from the milk of cattle grazing in verdant mountain pastures. Even the pasta of the North is rich—often made with eggs and dressed with a velvety cream sauce.

Clockwise from left: Linguine with Leeks & Peppers (see recipe, page 16), Mediterranean Eggplant & Cheese Casserole (see recipe, page 21) and Saffron "Butterflies" & Shrimp (see recipe, page 33).

Fettuccine with Rosy Tomato & Cream Sauce

FETTUCCINE CON SUGO ROSA

MAKES 6 TO 8 SERVINGS

- 3 tablespoons chopped fresh or 1 teaspoon dried basil leaves
- 1 tablespoon olive oil
- 1 (26-ounce) jar Classico® di Capri (Sun-Dried Tomato) Pasta Sauce
- 1 cup (½ pint) whipping cream or evaporated skim milk
- 2 tablespoons chopped fresh Italian parsley
- 1 (1-pound) package Classico® Fettuccine, cooked as package directs and drained

In saucepan, over medium heat, cook basil in oil 1 minute. Stir in pasta sauce, cream and parsley. Bring to a boil; reduce heat and simmer 10 minutes. Serve over hot fettuccine. Refrigerate leftovers.

Penne Gorgonzola

PENNE GORGONZOLA

MAKES 4 SERVINGS

- ½ (1-pound) package Classico® Penne Rigate, cooked as package directs and drained
- 2 cups (1 pint) half-and-half
- 1 cup (4 ounces) finely crumbled Gorgonzola cheese
- 4 ounces thinly sliced prosciutto ham, cut into 1-inch strips
- ½ cup chopped fresh Italian parsley

In Dutch oven, over medium heat, slowly bring half-and-half to a boil; boil 5 minutes. Gently whisk Gorgonzola cheese into boiling half-and-half; cook and stir until sauce is smooth and creamy. Add hot cooked penne, ham and parsley; mix well. Heat through. Serve immediately. Refrigerate leftovers.

Tuscan Pasta & Bean Soup *Toscana*
PASTA E FAGIOLI TOSCANA

MAKES 4 TO 6 SERVINGS

¾ **cup chopped onion**
2 **medium carrots, finely chopped (about 1 cup)**
½ **cup chopped celery**
2 **cloves garlic, chopped**
2 **tablespoons olive oil**
8 **cups water**
2 **tablespoons chicken-flavor bouillon granules**
¼ **to ½ teaspoon freshly ground black pepper**
1 **bay leaf**
½ **(1-pound) package Classico® Penne Rigate**
   or Gnocchi, uncooked
1 **(19-ounce) can cannellini beans, drained and rinsed**
2 **tablespoons chopped fresh Italian parsley**

In Dutch oven, over medium heat, cook and stir onion, carrots, celery
and garlic in oil until tender. Stir in water, bouillon, pepper and bay
leaf. Bring to a boil; reduce heat and simmer, covered, 20 minutes.
Add uncooked penne; cook 15 minutes longer or until tender, stirring
occasionally. Meanwhile, in blender or food processor, blend *half* the
beans until smooth. Stir mashed and whole beans into soup; heat
through. Remove bay leaf. Garnish with parsley. Refrigerate leftovers.

As with many
things Italian,
the story of the
origin of Gorgonzola
cheese is as rich as
the cheese itself.
In ancient Roman
times, cowherds and
shepherds would
stop at Gorgonzola—
a tiny town just
10 miles from
Milan—to rest their
weary feet on their
annual trek from
the lush mountain
grazing pastures
to the plains.
Gorgonzola found
itself awash in milk
it could not possibly
drink, so the
enterprising
townspeople turned
the surplus into the
creamy, tangy,
Gorgonzola blue
cheese that is
prized today.

Rigatoni & Cheese Casserole with Pesto

 *Emilia-Romagna*

RIGATONI E FORMAGGIO CON PESTO

MAKES 10 TO 12 SERVINGS

- 1 **pound lean ground beef**
- 2 **(26-ounce) jars Classico® di Genoa (Tomato & Pesto) Pasta Sauce**
- 1½ **teaspoons dried Italian seasoning**
- 1 **(15- or 16-ounce) container ricotta cheese**
- 4 **cups (1 pound) shredded mozzarella cheese**
- ¼ **cup freshly grated Parmesan cheese**
- 2 **eggs**
- 1 **(1-pound) package Classico® Rigatoni, cooked as package directs and drained**

Preheat oven to 350°. In saucepan, over medium heat, brown beef; pour off fat. Add pasta sauce and Italian seasoning. Cover; simmer 20 minutes. Combine ricotta cheese, *1 cup* mozzarella cheese, Parmesan cheese and eggs. On bottom of lightly greased 13x9-inch baking dish, spread *1 cup* pasta sauce mixture. Top with *half each* of the cooked rigatoni, ricotta cheese mixture and pasta sauce mixture. Sprinkle remaining *3 cups* mozzarella cheese over top. Repeat layering, ending with pasta sauce mixture. Bake, uncovered, until bubbly, 45 minutes. Let stand 15 minutes. Garnish with additional Parmesan cheese and fresh basil. Refrigerate leftovers.

Asparagus with Parmesan Cheese

Snap off and discard woody bases from 1 pound *fresh asparagus spears*. Cook, covered, in a small amount of boiling water until tender-crisp, 8 to 10 minutes; drain. Place asparagus in serving dish. Stir together 2 tablespoons *butter or margarine*, melted; ½ teaspoon finely grated *lemon rind* and ¼ teaspoon *cracked black pepper*. Pour over asparagus. Garnish with *lemon slices*. Sprinkle with freshly grated *Parmesan cheese*, if desired. Refrigerate leftovers. Makes 4 servings.

Italians often serve *biscotti,* twice-baked, semi-sweet cookies, for a mid-morning treat with coffee or cappuccino. But these light and crispy cookies, which are made expressly to be dipped in a drink of some kind, can be an ethereal end to a dinner as well. Try them with a sweet white wine such as Vino Santo or Marsala. Biscotti made with nuts, such as almonds, hazelnuts or pistachios, are the most common.

Country Garden Capellini *Lombardia*
CAPELLINI GIARDINIERA
MAKES 6 TO 8 SERVINGS

¼   **cup olive oil**
1   **(1½-pound) savoy cabbage, thinly sliced**
1   **pound carrots, cut into 2-inch thin strips**
1   **medium yellow onion, thinly sliced**
1   **(26-ounce) jar Classico® di Milano (Garden Zucchini & Parmesan) Pasta Sauce**
1   **(1-pound) package Classico® Capellini, cooked as package directs and drained**

In Dutch oven, over medium-high heat, heat oil; stir in vegetables. Cook and stir until vegetables are tender-crisp, about 2 minutes. Stir in pasta sauce, then capellini; heat through. Refrigerate leftovers.

Linguine with Leeks & Peppers *Liguria*
LINGUINE CON PORRI E PEPERONI
MAKES 6 TO 8 SERVINGS

1   **(1-pound) package Classico® Linguine, cooked as package directs and drained**
3   **medium leeks, cut in half lengthwise, then cut crosswise into ¼-inch pieces**
3   **cloves garlic, chopped**
1½   **teaspoons dried Italian seasoning**
⅓   **cup olive oil**
1   **(12-ounce) jar roasted red bell peppers, drained and sliced**
¼   **cup chopped fresh Italian parsley**
1   **cup (4 ounces) crumbled Gorgonzola cheese**

In Dutch oven, over medium heat, cook leeks, garlic and Italian seasoning in oil until tender. Stir in peppers; cook 2 minutes. Stir in cooked linguine and parsley; heat through. Season with salt and pepper. Sprinkle with cheese. Refrigerate leftovers.

Pictured on pages 10–11.

Polenta Soufflé

Piemonte

POLENTA SOUFFLÉ PIEMONTESE

MAKES 6 TO 8 SERVINGS

1 tablespoon Italian-seasoned bread crumbs
1 cup coarsely chopped onion
4 cloves garlic, chopped
2 tablespoons butter or margarine
3 cups water
¾ teaspoon salt
1½ cups white cornmeal
1 (26-ounce) jar Classico® di Parma (Four Cheese) or
   di Firenze (Florentine Spinach & Cheese) Pasta Sauce
¾ teaspoon freshly ground black pepper
4 eggs
   Freshly grated Parmesan cheese

Preheat oven to 375°. Generously butter 8- or 9-inch square baking dish; sprinkle lightly with bread crumbs. In large saucepan, over medium heat, cook onion and garlic in butter until tender. Stir in water and salt. Bring to a boil; gradually beat in cornmeal with wire whisk until well blended. Reduce heat to medium-low; cook and stir 5 minutes. Remove from heat; stir in *2 cups* pasta sauce and pepper. Beat in eggs. Turn into prepared baking dish. Bake until set, about 50 minutes. Heat remaining pasta sauce. Serve sauce over warm soufflé topped with Parmesan cheese. Refrigerate leftovers.

In the region of Piemonte, a hot bath is good with dinner. *Bagna calda* is a "hot bath" of extra-virgin olive oil, butter, chopped garlic cloves (at least one per diner) and a few finely chopped anchovies. The mixture is kept warm over a small flame (a fondue pot works well) for dipping raw vegetables. This famous Piemontese sauce served with vegetables is the perfect accompani-

Lasagne Florentine *Toscana*

LASAGNE FIORENTINA

MAKES 10 TO 12 SERVINGS

¾ **cup chopped onion**

2 **cloves garlic, chopped**

2 **tablespoons olive oil**

2 **(26-ounce) jars Classico® di Firenze (Florentine Spinach & Cheese) Pasta Sauce**

1 **(15- or 16-ounce) container ricotta cheese**

4 **cups (1 pound) shredded mozzarella cheese**

⅓ **cup freshly grated Parmesan cheese**

2 **eggs**

1 **(1-pound) package lasagne noodles, cooked as package directs and drained**

Fresh spinach leaves

Preheat oven to 350°. In large saucepan, over medium heat, cook onion and garlic in oil until tender. Add pasta sauce; simmer, uncovered, 15 minutes. In medium bowl, combine ricotta cheese, *½ cup* mozzarella cheese, Parmesan cheese and eggs. In 15x9-inch baking dish, layer *2 cups* sauce, *half* of the cooked lasagne noodles, *half* of the remaining sauce, all of the ricotta cheese mixture, *half* of the remaining mozzarella cheese, the remaining lasagne noodles and the remaining sauce. Bake, covered, until hot and bubbly, 45 minutes. Uncover; top with remaining mozzarella cheese. Bake 15 minutes longer. Let stand 15 minutes. Garnish with fresh spinach leaves. Refrigerate leftovers.

*T*he term *florentine* is actually a French word, meaning "on a bed of spinach." In common use, florentine simply means the dish uses spinach in some form. In the 16th century, when Catherine de Medici of the famed Florentine family married the King of France, she imported her personal chefs to France. It was there the chefs first encountered fresh spinach. They were apparently so enamored with it that any dish containing spinach took on the name of the illustrious Renaissance city.

Baked Penne with Artichokes & Peas  *Valle d'Aosta*

PENNE CON CARCIOFI E PISELLI VENEZIANA

MAKES 10 TO 12 SERVINGS

1	(9-ounce) package frozen artichoke hearts, thawed and chopped
2	cloves garlic, chopped
¼	cup plus 3 tablespoons butter or margarine
1	pound plum tomatoes, chopped and drained
1	(10-ounce) package frozen green peas, thawed
4	teaspoons chicken-flavor bouillon granules
3	tablespoons flour
2½	cups milk
¾	cup freshly grated Parmesan cheese
1	(1-pound) package Classico® Penne Rigate, cooked as package directs and drained
1	cup (4 ounces) shredded fontina cheese

Preheat oven to 350°. In large skillet, over medium heat, cook and stir artichokes and garlic in *3 tablespoons* butter until hot and garlic is tender. Stir in tomatoes; cook and stir 5 minutes. Stir in peas and *2 teaspoons* bouillon. Set aside. In medium saucepan, melt remaining *¼ cup* butter; stir in flour, remaining *2 teaspoons* bouillon and milk. Cook and stir until thickened and bubbly. Stir in *¼ cup* Parmesan cheese. Spread *one-third* of the cheese sauce on bottom of greased 13x9-inch baking dish. Top with *half each* of the cooked penne and the tomato mixture. Top with *half* of the remaining cheese sauce, *½ cup* fontina cheese and *¼ cup* Parmesan cheese. Repeat layering, ending with remaining *¼ cup* Parmesan cheese. Bake, uncovered, until hot and bubbly, about 30 minutes. Refrigerate leftovers.

To prepare a fresh artichoke, wash it, then cut off the bottom stem so the artichoke sits flat. Cut off 1 inch from the top. Remove loose outer leaves. Snip off ½ inch from tips of remaining leaves. Brush the cut surfaces with lemon juice. Boil in enough salted water to cover for 20 to 30 minutes. Invert to drain. To eat, pull outer leaves off one at a time and dip into melted butter. When fleshy outer leaves have been pulled off, remove thin inner leaves, exposing the fuzzy "choke." Scoop out choke and discard.

Mediterranean Eggplant & Cheese Casserole

Sardegna

MELANZANE TRE FORMAGGI AL FORNO

MAKES 8 TO 10 SERVINGS

1	medium eggplant, cut into small cubes (about 6 cups)
1	cup chopped onion
4	cloves garlic, finely chopped
⅓	cup olive oil
1	(26-ounce) jar Classico® di Napoli (Tomato & Basil) Pasta Sauce
½	cup sliced ripe olives
¼	cup capers, drained
½	to 1 teaspoon dried red pepper flakes
1	(15- or 16-ounce) container ricotta cheese
¼	cup milk
1	(1-pound) package Classico® Fusilli, cooked as package directs and drained
3	cups (¾ pound) shredded mozzarella cheese
½	cup freshly grated pecorino Romano cheese
	Sautéed eggplant slices
	Fresh Italian parsley

Preheat oven to 350°. In Dutch oven, over medium-high heat, cook and stir eggplant cubes, onion and garlic in oil until tender. Stir in pasta sauce, olives, capers and red pepper flakes. Bring to a boil; reduce heat and simmer, covered, 20 minutes. Meanwhile, in large bowl, combine ricotta cheese and milk; mix well. Stir in cooked fusilli. On bottom of greased 13x9-inch baking dish, layer *one-third each* of the eggplant mixture, pasta mixture, mozzarella cheese and Romano cheese. Repeat layers twice. Bake, covered, 20 minutes. Bake, uncovered, 20 minutes longer or until hot and bubbly. Garnish with eggplant slices and parsley. Refrigerate leftovers.

Pictured on pages 10–11.

Mild- and delicately-flavored mozzarella cheese, synonymous with pizza and baked pasta dishes, hails from Campania—particularly Naples—where it was first made from the milk of Indian water buffalo. Today most mozzarella cheese is made from cow's milk. It will be trumpeted as *mozzarella di bufalo* if it is the genuine article. Mozzarella aficionados insist it should be eaten fresh, when it is still very soft, but most mozzarella is aged so it will keep better.

Grilled Chicken & Penne Salad

INSALATA DI POLLO ALLA GRIGLIA

MAKES 4 TO 6 SERVINGS

- 1 pound skinned, boneless chicken breast halves
  Salt and pepper
- ¼ cup lemon juice
- ½ (1-pound) package Classico® Penne Rigate, cooked as package directs and drained
- 3 medium plum tomatoes, chopped
- 1 cup (4 ounces) crumbled Gorgonzola cheese
- ½ cup sliced ripe olives
- 1 teaspoon dried Italian seasoning
  Italian Salad Dressing
- 1 cup coarsely chopped watercress
  Assorted tomatoes

Season chicken lightly with salt and pepper. Grill or broil until lightly browned and chicken is no longer pink, basting with lemon juice. Slice chicken; cover and chill. In large bowl, combine cooked penne, plum tomatoes, Gorgonzola cheese, olives and Italian seasoning; mix well. Prepare Italian Salad Dressing; stir into salad. Cover; chill thoroughly. Just before serving, stir in watercress; top with chicken. Garnish with assorted tomatoes. Refrigerate leftovers.

Italian Salad Dressing: In small bowl, combine ¾ cup *olive oil*, 3 tablespoons *white wine vinegar* or *balsamic vinegar*, 1 teaspoon *dry mustard* or 2 teaspoons *Dijon-style mustard*, 1 teaspoon *dried Italian seasoning*, 1 teaspoon *salt* and ½ teaspoon *freshly ground black pepper*; mix well.

In Italy, salads are dressed simply using the very best oils and vinegars. Balsamic vinegar, or *aceto balsamico,* is one of those and can be substituted for the white wine vinegar in the dressing at left. True aceto balsamico is made in the city of Modena in Emilia-Romagna. It is a thick, dark vinegar flavored with herbs and aged like wine for a minimum of 12 years in a succession of oak, chestnut, mulberry and juniper-wood barrels—each of which contributes to its sweet flavor and fragrance.

Gnocchi with Chicken & Four-Cheese Sauce

 Umbria

GNOCCHI E POLLO CON QUATTRO FORMAGGI
MAKES 6 TO 8 SERVINGS

1	to 1½ pounds skinned, boneless chicken breast halves, cooked and sliced into 2-inch strips
1	cup chopped onion
3	cloves garlic, chopped
¼	cup olive oil
2	tablespoons chopped fresh Italian parsley
1	tablespoon chopped fresh or ½ teaspoon dried rosemary leaves
2	(26-ounce) jars Classico® di Parma (Four Cheese) Pasta Sauce
¼	teaspoon freshly ground black pepper
1	(1-pound) package Classico® Gnocchi, cooked as package directs and drained
	Chopped green onions

In Dutch oven, over medium heat, cook 1 cup onion and garlic in oil until tender. Add chicken, parsley and rosemary; cook and stir 6 to 8 minutes. Add pasta sauce and pepper. Bring to a boil; reduce heat and simmer 15 minutes. In large serving bowl, place hot cooked gnocchi. Add sauce and toss. Garnish with green onions. Refrigerate leftovers.

Zabaglione*

In the top of a double boiler, beat 3 *egg yolks* and ⅓ cup *dry Marsala* or *cream sherry* until well blended. Stir in ¼ cup *sugar* and dash *salt*. Place over *boiling water* (upper pan should not touch the water). Beat with an electric mixer on high speed for 7 to 8 minutes or until mixture thickens and mounds. Serve immediately in stemmed glasses or over *fresh fruit*, if desired. Refrigerate leftovers. Makes 4 servings.

***Note:** Zabaglione is a foamy custard.

---

*G*rilled bread— *bruschetta* in some parts of Italy and *fettunta* in others— often opens a meal. Simply cut Italian country bread into thick slices, grill or broil the slices, then rub with a peeled, cut garlic clove and brush with some extra-virgin olive oil. Bruschetta can be topped with chopped tomatoes, fresh basil and olive oil; white beans marinated in olive oil, garlic and freshly ground black pepper; or some chopped fresh herbs, such as basil or oregano leaves.

Chicken Florentine with Mushrooms & Penne

 Toscana

POLLO FIORENTINA

MAKES 4 TO 6 SERVINGS

1	(3-pound) cut-up broiler-fryer chicken or chicken parts
	Salt and pepper
	Flour
3	tablespoons olive oil
1	cup sliced fresh mushrooms
2	cloves garlic, chopped
1	(26-ounce) jar Classico® di Firenze (Florentine Spinach & Cheese) Pasta Sauce
1	tablespoon chopped fresh or 1 teaspoon dried rosemary leaves
1	(1-pound) package Classico® Penne Rigate, cooked as package directs and drained

Season chicken with salt and pepper; coat lightly with flour. In large nonstick skillet or Dutch oven, over medium heat, brown chicken in oil. Remove chicken from skillet; drain on paper towels. Add mushrooms and garlic to drippings; cook and stir, over medium heat, until tender. Stir in pasta sauce and rosemary. Top with chicken pieces. Bring to a boil; reduce heat and simmer, covered, until chicken is no longer pink, about 25 minutes. Serve over hot cooked penne. Refrigerate leftovers.

hianti, the most famous Italian wine, is a dry, fruity red wine that is synonymous with Toscana and its simple, earthy foods. Its production is strictly regulated by Italian law, which stipulates it be made from four varieties of grapes—two red and two white. To ensure quality when selecting a Chianti, check for the words "Chianti Classico" on the label. Another way to identify a quality Chianti is to look for a picture of a black rooster or a cherub on a label glued to the neck of the bottle.

Next to family and faith, nothing is more important to an Italian than a good home-cooked meal. Even today, the average Italian eats out only a little more than 10 times in a year. Breakfast is not of great import—it usually consists of an espresso and maybe a few biscotti—but *pranzo* (lunch) and *cena* (dinner) highlight the day. School-age children and working fathers all return home to eat their most substantial meal of the day between 12:30 and 2 p.m. The lighter meal, *cena,* is taken between 7:30 and 10 p.m.

Venetian Chicken in Spicy Tomato Cream

POLLO VENEZIANA CON POMODORI PANNA

MAKES 4 TO 6 SERVINGS

1   **pound skinned, boneless chicken breast halves, cut into 1-inch pieces**
3   **tablespoons chopped fresh or 1 teaspoon dried basil leaves**
2   **tablespoons olive oil**
1   **(26-ounce) jar Classico® di Roma Arrabbiata (Spicy Red Pepper) Pasta Sauce**
½   **cup whipping cream or evaporated skim milk**
2   **tablespoons chopped fresh Italian parsley**
1   **(1-pound) package Classico® Penne Rigate, cooked as package directs and drained**

Season chicken lightly with salt and pepper. In Dutch oven, over medium-high heat, cook and stir chicken and basil in oil until chicken is no longer pink. Stir in pasta sauce, cream and parsley. Bring to a boil; reduce heat and simmer, covered, 10 minutes. Serve with hot cooked penne, and garnish with parsley. Refrigerate leftovers.

Gorgonzola & Walnut Flat Bread

Thaw 1 (1-pound) loaf *frozen bread dough*; divide into 6 portions. Cover; let rest 10 minutes. Cook 3 medium *onions*, thinly sliced and separated into rings, in 3 tablespoons *olive oil* until very tender but not brown; set aside. Cover 4 dough portions; chill. Roll remaining 2 portions into 8-inch rounds; place on a greased baking sheet. Using ¾ cup finely chopped *walnuts*, top *each* round with *one-sixth* of the walnuts. Top *each* round with *one-sixth* of the onion mixture. Cover; let rise in a warm place for 15 minutes. Preheat oven to 450°. Bake 8 minutes. Using 1 cup crumbled *Gorgonzola cheese*, sprinkle *one-sixth* of the cheese on each round. Bake rounds 4 to 6 minutes longer or until crisp and golden. Repeat rolling, topping, rising and baking with the remaining ingredients. Makes 6 rounds or 12 servings.

With the exception of the high Alps, Italy is one great olive grove. Each region grows its own type of olives, thus producing oils with unique characteristics. Ligurian olive oil is the lightest. Tuscan oils and oils produced in the South are much darker and more intensely flavored and aromatic. Reserve the most costly extra-virgin olive oils for salad dressings and to drizzle in soups and on pastas and meats for flavor. Virgin or pure olive oils are a better choice for cooking.

Simmered Chicken with Peppers & Provolone

POLLO CON PEPERONI E PROVOLONE

MAKES 4 SERVINGS

4   skinned, boneless chicken breast halves (about 1 pound)
    Salt and pepper
    Flour
2   cloves garlic, finely chopped
3   tablespoons olive oil
1   (26-ounce) jar Classico® di Genoa (Tomato & Pesto) or
        di Milano (Garden Zucchini & Parmesan) Pasta Sauce
1   small green bell pepper, cut into strips
1   small red bell pepper, cut into strips
2   slices provolone cheese, cut in half
½   (1-pound) package Classico® Farfalle, cooked as package
        directs and drained
    Chopped fresh Italian parsley

Season chicken lightly with salt and pepper; coat with flour. In large skillet, over medium-high heat, brown chicken and garlic in *2 tablespoons* oil; remove chicken from skillet. Add pasta sauce, then top with chicken. Bring to a boil; reduce heat. Simmer, covered, 20 minutes, adding peppers during last 5 minutes. Uncover; top each chicken breast half with *half* provolone cheese slice. Toss hot cooked farfalle with remaining *1 tablespoon* oil and parsley; serve with chicken and sauce. Refrigerate leftovers.

Chicken Marengo

Piemonte

POLLO MARENGO PIEMONTESE

MAKES 4 TO 6 SERVINGS

1	(3-pound) cut-up broiler-fryer chicken
	Salt and pepper
	Flour
¼	cup olive oil
½	pound sliced fresh mushrooms
2	tablespoons chopped fresh or 1 teaspoon dried basil leaves
4	cloves garlic, chopped
¼	cup dry white vermouth or wine
1	(26-ounce) jar Classico® di Napoli (Tomato & Basil) Pasta Sauce
½	pound raw large shrimp, peeled and deveined
3	tablespoons chopped fresh Italian parsley

Season chicken lightly with salt and pepper; coat with flour. In large skillet, over medium-high heat, brown chicken in oil. Remove from skillet. Pour off all but *1 tablespoon* drippings from skillet. Over medium-high heat, cook and stir mushrooms, basil and garlic in drippings until mushrooms are tender. Stir in vermouth; boil 2 minutes. Stir in pasta sauce; return the chicken to skillet. Bring to a boil; reduce heat and simmer until chicken is no longer pink, about 20 minutes. Top with shrimp; simmer, covered, until shrimp are pink. Garnish with parsley. Refrigerate leftovers.

Zesty Green Beans

Cook 1 (9-ounce) package *frozen Italian-style green beans* according to package directions; drain. Set aside. In a small saucepan, over medium heat, melt 1 tablespoon *butter or margarine*. Add ⅓ cup sliced *green onions* and 1 clove *garlic,* finely chopped; cook and stir until onions are tender. Add 1 ounce *salami,* cut into thin strips; 2 tablespoons *red wine vinegar;* 1 tablespoon chopped *fresh Italian parsley* and dash *freshly ground black pepper.* Cook and stir 1 minute. Stir in beans; heat through. Refrigerate leftovers. Makes 4 servings.

As an antipasto for the fragrant and classic Piemontese dinner featured on this page, try wrapping paper-thin slices of prosciutto ham around thin half-moons of melon, such as cantaloupe, or—when they're in season—peeled and quartered fresh figs.

Linguine with Creamy Clam & Mushroom Sauce

LINGUINE E VONGOLE ADRIATICA

MAKES 4 SERVINGS

½ **pound sliced fresh mushrooms**
⅓ **cup finely chopped onion**
1 **clove garlic, finely chopped**
2 **to 3 tablespoons olive oil or butter**
2 **tablespoons flour**
1 **(8-ounce) bottle clam juice***
1 **cup (½ pint) half-and-half or evaporated skim milk**
1 **to 2 teaspoons chicken-flavor bouillon granules**
1 **cup frozen green peas, thawed**
¼ **cup freshly grated Parmesan cheese**
1 **tablespoon dry white vermouth or wine**
½ **(1-pound) package Classico® Linguine, cooked as package directs and drained**
2 **dozen cockle,** **cherrystone or littleneck clams, cleaned and steamed**
Lemon wedges

In Dutch oven, over medium-high heat, cook and stir mushrooms, onion and garlic in oil until liquid from mushrooms is absorbed. Reduce heat to medium; stir in flour. Gradually stir in clam juice, half-and-half and bouillon; cook and stir until thickened. Add peas, Parmesan cheese and vermouth; mix well. Heat through *(do not boil)*. Serve over hot cooked linguine with hot steamed clams and lemon wedges. Refrigerate leftovers.

***Note:** Two (6½-ounce) cans chopped or minced *clams*, drained (reserving liquid) can be substituted for fresh steamed clams and clam juice. Add drained clams with the peas, Parmesan cheese and vermouth. Proceed as directed above.

****Note:** Cockles, the New Zealand variety of clams shown opposite, exhibit a distinctive green color. These clams are quite small and are typically sweeter than other varieties.

When you buy live, fresh clams, look for moist shells without cracks or chips. Only buy clams that close when gently tapped. To prepare clams, use a stiff brush to scrub clam shells under cold running water, ridding them of any sand. To steam, fill an 8-quart Dutch oven with ½ inch of water; bring to boiling. Place clams in a steamer basket in the Dutch oven. Cover and steam until shells open and clams are cooked, about 5 to 7 minutes. Discard any that do not open.

Linguine with Creamy Clam & Mushroom Sauce

Spaghetti with Shrimp & Fresh Basil *Liguria*

SPAGHETTI CON GAMBERI GENOVESE

MAKES 6 TO 8 SERVINGS

¾   **cup chopped onion**
4   **cloves garlic, finely chopped**
3   **tablespoons butter or margarine**
¾   **cup firmly packed fresh basil leaves, chopped (about 1½ ounces)**
½   **cup dry white vermouth or wine**
2   **tablespoons roux (1 tablespoon butter melted and mixed with 1 tablespoon flour)**
1   **tablespoon tomato paste**
1   **cup (½ pint) whipping cream**
1   **pound raw medium shrimp, peeled and deveined**
    Salt and pepper
1   **(1-pound) package Classico® Spaghetti, cooked as package directs and drained**
    Freshly grated Parmesan cheese

In Dutch oven, over medium heat, cook onion and garlic in *1 tablespoon* butter until tender. Add basil; cook and stir for 1 minute. Stir in vermouth. Cook 8 minutes or until mixture is reduced by one-third. Stir in roux and tomato paste; cook 5 minutes longer. Add cream; bring to a boil. Reduce heat and simmer 5 minutes. Remove from heat; set aside. Season shrimp lightly with salt and pepper. In large skillet, over medium-high heat, cook and stir shrimp in remaining *2 tablespoons* butter until shrimp are pink; drain. To Dutch oven with sauce, add cooked spaghetti; mix well. Heat through; transfer to a serving platter. To serve, arrange shrimp on top or toss with spaghetti and sauce. Serve with Parmesan cheese. Refrigerate leftovers.

A Ligurian salad—like all Italian salads—changes with the seasons, but its greens and vegetables are always dressed simply. On Liguria's coast, a typical vegetable salad may consist of shredded red cabbage and radicchio with julienned carrots and fennel dressed with local olive oil, white wine vinegar, salt, white pepper and a sprinkle of chopped fresh herbs. Such a salad would make a fine accompaniment to this shrimp dish.

Saffron "Butterflies" & Shrimp *Abruzzi*

FARFALLE E GAMBERI ZAFFERANO

MAKES 8 TO 10 SERVINGS

- 1 (1-pound) package Classico® Farfalle, cooked as package directs and drained
- 1 pound fresh asparagus, trimmed and cut into 1-inch pieces and steamed
- ¾ cup dry white vermouth
- ¼ to ½ teaspoon saffron
- 1½ pounds raw medium shrimp, peeled and deveined
- 2 tablespoons olive oil
- ¼ cup finely chopped shallots
- 2 cups (1 pint) half-and-half
- 2 teaspoons chicken-flavor bouillon granules
- ¼ cup chopped fresh chives

In 1-cup glass measure, combine vermouth and saffron; let stand 15 minutes. In large skillet, over medium heat, cook and stir shrimp in oil until shrimp are pink. Remove from skillet. In same skillet, combine vermouth mixture and shallots. Bring to a boil; continue boiling rapidly until most of the liquid is absorbed, about 4 minutes. Stir in half-and-half and bouillon. Bring to a boil; boil 5 minutes or until thickened, stirring constantly. Stir in cooked farfalle, asparagus and shrimp; heat through. Top with chives. Serve immediately. Refrigerate leftovers.

Pictured on pages 10–11.

The most expensive spice in the world, saffron, was so prized by the Venetians for its flavor, aroma and amber color, an Office of Saffron was set up in the 12th century to manage the trade of this exquisite spice. Saffron is the dried stigmas of the saffron crocus—a flower that thrives in the Abruzzi region. Saffron continues to be a precious spice because it must be harvested by hand, beginning at dawn, before the heat from the sun wilts the flowers.

Penne with Blushing Shrimp Pesto *Liguria*
PENNE ALLA PORTOFINO
MAKES 6 TO 8 SERVINGS

1	**pound small raw shrimp, peeled, deveined and cooked**
½	**to ¾ cup slivered almonds**
½	**to ¾ cup olive oil**
4	**cloves garlic, chopped**
1	**teaspoon freshly ground black pepper**
1	**teaspoon salt**
1	**(26-ounce) jar Classico® di Genoa (Tomato & Pesto) Pasta Sauce**
1	**(1-pound) package Classico® Penne Rigate, cooked as package directs and drained**
	Fresh basil leaves

Reserve 6 to 8 shrimp for garnish. In food processor or blender, combine remaining shrimp, almonds, oil, garlic, pepper and salt; blend until smooth. In medium saucepan, over medium heat, combine shrimp mixture and pasta sauce; heat through. In large pasta bowl, toss shrimp mixture with hot cooked penne. Garnish with reserved shrimp and basil; serve immediately. Refrigerate leftovers.

egend has it that Genoese sailors popularized pesto, the aromatic Ligurian sauce of ground fresh basil, garlic, olive oil, pecorino Romano cheese, Parmesan cheese and pine nuts. Presumably, pesto had the earthy, green freshness they yearned for on their long sea journeys. In Liguria, pesto flavors pasta and gives the loved minestrone—*minestrone alla genovese*—its distinctive flavor and color.

Penne with Blushing Shrimp Pesto

A light and refreshing dessert to cap this rich meal might be *macedonia*. This compote of fresh fruits, such as peaches, cherries, apples and figs—all of which are plentiful in the region of Marche from spring through fall—is soaked in a little fruit brandy and sugar for 2 to 3 hours in the refrigerator before serving.

Fettuccine with Scallops & Creamy Mushroom Sauce

Fettuccine e Cappe Sante con Panna

Makes 6 to 8 servings

½ **pound sliced fresh mushrooms**
¾ **cup finely chopped onion**
1 **clove garlic, chopped**
2 **to 3 tablespoons olive oil or butter**
2 **tablespoons flour**
2 **cups (1 pint) half-and-half**
2 **teaspoons chicken-flavor bouillon granules**
¼ **cup freshly grated Parmesan cheese**
1 **tablespoon dry white vermouth or wine**
1 **pound bay scallops**
1 **(1-pound) package Classico® Fettuccine, cooked as package directs and drained**

In large saucepan, over medium-high heat, cook and stir mushrooms, onion and garlic in oil until liquid from mushrooms is absorbed. Reduce heat to medium; stir in flour. Gradually stir in half-and-half, then bouillon; cook and stir until thickened. Stir in Parmesan cheese, vermouth and scallops; cook and stir until scallops are opaque and mixture is hot *(do not boil)*. Serve immediately over hot cooked fettuccine. Refrigerate leftovers.

Peas with Prosciutto

In large skillet, over medium-high heat, cook and stir 1 small *red onion,* cut into thin wedges, and 2 ounces *prosciutto ham,* cut into thin strips, in 1 tablespoon *olive oil* until onion is tender but not brown. Add 1 (10-ounce) package *frozen green peas,* ½ cup *water* and ⅛ teaspoon *freshly ground black pepper.* Bring to a boil; boil gently, uncovered, until peas are tender and most of the liquid is absorbed, 8 to 10 minutes. Refrigerate leftovers. Makes 4 servings.

Emerald Coast Lobster & Capellini with Lemon Butter

Sardegna

ASTICE ALLA COSTA SMERELDA

MAKES 4 SERVINGS

Lemon Butter Sauce
1 (1-pound) package Classico® Capellini, cooked as package directs and drained
1 pound fresh pea pods, cut into strips and blanched 1 minute
½ pound carrots, cut into strips and blanched 2 minutes
2 (1 to 1½ pound) lobsters, cooked and split lengthwise
4 tablespoons olive oil
¼ cup sliced or chopped ripe olives

Prepare Lemon Butter Sauce. In large pasta bowl, toss together hot cooked capellini, pea pods, carrots and ½ *cup* Lemon Butter Sauce. Cover and keep warm. In large skillet, over medium-high heat, cook each lobster half, meat-side down, in 1 *tablespoon* oil for 2 minutes. To serve, arrange *one-fourth* of the capellini mixture on each serving plate; top *each* serving with a lobster half (still in shell). Garnish with olives and serve with remaining Lemon Butter Sauce. Refrigerate leftovers.

Lemon Butter Sauce: In medium saucepan, combine 1¼ cups *dry white vermouth or wine* and ½ cup finely chopped *onion*. Bring to a boil; boil 3 minutes. Stir in 2 tablespoons *whipping cream*, then ¾ cup *butter*, 2 tablespoons *lemon juice* and 1 teaspoon grated *lemon rind*. Cook and stir until butter is melted and mixture is thick and creamy, about 2 minutes. Remove from heat; stir in ¼ cup chopped *fresh chives*.

Lobster is something of a Sardegnan specialty. Scant along the coasts of mainland Italy, lobsters are plentiful in Sardegna where they are served in the elegant resorts of the *Costa Smerelda* (Emerald Coast) and exported to the rest of Italy. In addition to being prepared with pasta, lobsters are often baked with lemon juice, olive oil, bread crumbs and herbs such as parsley and basil.

Abruzzi Bean, Rice & Cheese Soup

ZUPPA D'ABRUZZI

MAKES 8 TO 10 SERVINGS

- 1 (1-pound) package dried great northern beans, sorted, rinsed, soaked 12 hours and drained
- 12 cups water
- 1 pound curly endive, rinsed, chopped and drained
- 1 cup chopped fresh or 2 tablespoons dried basil leaves
- 1 cup chopped fresh Italian parsley
- 1/3 cup chopped fresh mint leaves
- 1/3 cup olive oil
- 1 tablespoon dried red pepper flakes
- 6 cloves garlic, chopped
- 2 teaspoons salt
- 1/4 teaspoon ground marjoram
- 1 (26-ounce) jar Classico® d'Abruzzi (Italian Sausage & Fennel) Pasta Sauce
- 1 cup uncooked arborio rice
- 1 (4-ounce) chunk pecorino Romano cheese, cut into small pieces
   Freshly shredded pecorino Romano cheese

In large kettle, combine beans, water, endive, basil, parsley, mint, oil, red pepper flakes, garlic, salt, and marjoram; mix well. Over medium-high heat, bring to a boil. Reduce heat and simmer, covered, until beans are tender, about 2 hours. Stir in pasta sauce and rice; cook 30 minutes longer or until rice is tender, stirring occasionally. Remove from heat; stir in 4 *ounces* Romano cheese pieces. Garnish with freshly shredded Romano cheese; serve immediately. Refrigerate leftovers.

ecorino is a sharply flavored, hard cheese made from sheep's milk. Most regions in central and southern Italy make their own version of pecorino, so there is pecorino Romano, pecorino toscano and pecorino sardo from Sardegna. Some Sicilian versions of pecorino are flavored with black peppercorns or saffron. But all pecorinos have one thing in common: They are aged 6 to 18 months, and they're all uncommonly delicious.

Fettuccine with Prosciutto, Peppers & Peas

Emilia-Romagna

FETTUCCINE ALLA PARMA

MAKES 6 TO 8 SERVINGS

½ **pound thinly sliced prosciutto ham, cut into small pieces**
1 **cup chopped onion**
1 **cup coarsely chopped red and yellow bell peppers**
2 **tablespoons chopped fresh or 1 teaspoon dried**
  thyme leaves
3 **tablespoons olive oil**
1 **(26-ounce) jar Classico® di Parma (Four Cheese) or**
  di Milano (Garden Zucchini & Parmesan) Pasta Sauce
1 **(10-ounce) package frozen green peas, thawed**
1 **(1-pound) package Classico® Fettuccine, cooked as package**
  directs and drained

In large saucepan, over medium-high heat, cook and stir ham, onion, peppers and thyme in oil until vegetables are tender. Reduce heat to medium. Add pasta sauce and peas; heat through. Serve over hot cooked fettuccine. Refrigerate leftovers.

Tuscan Bread Salad

In large bowl, stir together 3 cups dry *Italian bread cubes;* 2 large ripe *tomatoes,* peeled and coarsely chopped; 1 small *red onion,* chopped; ⅓ cup sliced, pitted *ripe olives* and ¼ cup chopped *fresh basil or oregano leaves.* For dressing, in screw-top jar, combine 3 tablespoons *olive oil;* 2 tablespoons *red wine vinegar;* 3 cloves *garlic,* finely chopped; ¼ teaspoon *salt* and ⅛ teaspoon *freshly ground black pepper.* Cover and shake until well blended. Pour over bread mixture. Serve immediately on *lettuce leaves.* Refrigerate leftovers. Makes 6 servings.

---

*T*he conclusion of a meal featuring this fettuccine dish could be a simple Italian dessert— fresh, light ricotta cheese sprinkled with sugar and one of these accompaniments: cocoa, cognac, fresh strawberries or even finely ground coffee. Serve a spoonful of the sweetened ricotta in a pretty ice-cream dish to each person.

Alpine Gnocchi with Ham & Fontina *Piemonte*

GNOCCHI VALDOSTANA

MAKES 6 TO 8 SERVINGS

1   (1-pound) package Classico® Gnocchi, cooked as package
    directs and drained
½   pound sliced fresh mushrooms
2   tablespoons chopped fresh basil leaves
4   cloves garlic, chopped
2   tablespoons butter or margarine
2   cups (1 pint) half-and-half or evaporated skim milk
¼   pound thinly sliced prosciutto ham, chopped
1   cup (4 ounces) shredded fontina cheese

In Dutch oven, over medium-high heat, cook and stir mushrooms,
basil and garlic in butter until liquid from mushrooms is absorbed.
Stir in half-and-half and ham. Bring to a boil; boil 5 minutes or until
thickened. Reduce heat to medium. Add fontina cheese; cook and stir
until melted. Stir in hot cooked gnocchi; heat through. Serve
immediately. Refrigerate leftovers.

There are almost as many ways to eat gnocchi as there are villages in Italy. The gnocchi of Emilia-Romagna are made with ricotta, spinach, eggs, Parmesan, wheat flour and a touch of nutmeg; the gnocchi of Rome are made with semolina—pasta flour; and the gnocchi of Venice are made with potatoes and dressed with butter and smoked ricotta. In the Alpine regions, gnocchi are adorned with butter or cream and fontina cheese.

Fettuccine with Country Ham & Walnuts *Liguria*

FETTUCCINE CON NOCI LIGURIANA

MAKES 6 TO 8 SERVINGS

1 (1-pound) package Classico® Fettuccine, cooked as package directs and drained
2 tablespoons finely chopped shallots
4 cloves garlic, finely chopped
2 tablespoons butter or margarine
3 cups (1½ pints) half-and-half
4 cups fresh spinach, rinsed, drained and coarsely chopped
½ pound country ham (fully baked or country cured), cut into thin 1-inch strips
½ cup chopped walnuts, lightly toasted
½ cup fresh basil leaves, chopped
½ cup freshly grated Parmesan cheese
⅓ cup warm water
1 teaspoon chicken-flavor bouillon granules

In Dutch oven, over medium-high heat, cook and stir shallots and garlic in butter until tender. Quickly add half-and-half; bring to a boil. Boil 1 minute. Stir in spinach, ham, walnuts, basil, Parmesan cheese, water and bouillon. Bring to a boil; reduce heat and simmer 3 minutes. Stir in cooked fettuccine. Cook and stir until heated through and creamy. Serve immediately. Refrigerate leftovers.

*talian foods are directly linked to the land from which they come. Many of the most prized ingredients in the Italian larder are named for their place of origination. There is Parma ham—prosciutto—from the area around Parma, Gorgonzola cheese produced in the town of Gorgonzola and Soave white wine from the village of Soave near Verona. These prized foods travel like delectable goodwill ambassadors to the rest of Italy and the world, bearing their locale names with pride.

Farfalle & Prosciutto in Parmesan Cream Sauce

FARFALLE E PROSCIUTTO ALLA PARMA

MAKES 6 TO 8 SERVINGS

1   (1-pound) package Classico® Farfalle, cooked as package
    directs and drained
6   ounces thinly sliced prosciutto ham, cut into 1-inch strips
¼   cup butter or margarine
1   cup half-and-half
1   cup freshly grated Parmesan cheese
1   cup frozen green peas, thawed

In Dutch oven, over medium-high heat, cook and stir ham in butter until lightly browned. Stir in half-and-half. Bring to a boil; boil 1½ minutes. Reduce heat to medium. Stir in Parmesan cheese until smooth. Add cooked farfalle and peas; mix well. Heat through. Serve immediately. Refrigerate leftovers.

Pear Crostata

Preheat oven to 450°. Unfold 2 piecrusts from 1 (15-ounce) package *refrigerated pie crust*; let stand according to package directions. Press 1 of the crusts into a 10- to 11-inch tart pan with removable bottom. Line with double thickness of foil. Bake 10 minutes. Remove from oven. Reduce oven temperature to 375°. In medium bowl, combine ¼ cup *sugar* and 1 tablespoon *all-purpose flour*. Add 4 cups sliced, peeled *pears*; toss to coat. Arrange pear slices in prebaked crust in tart pan. Spoon ⅔ cup *apricot preserves* evenly over pears. Cut remaining crust into ½-inch-wide strips. Arrange strips over pears in a lattice pattern. Trim strips to edges of pan. Beat 1 *egg* with 1 tablespoon *water*; brush on lattice. Sprinkle with 1 tablespoon *sugar*. Bake until fruit is tender, 45 to 50 minutes. To prevent overbrowning, cover loosely with foil the last 10 to 15 minutes. Serve warm with *whipped cream*. Makes 8 to 10 servings.

One of Italy's oldest cheeses is also its most ubiquitous. Parmesan appears in antipasto and is grated over pasta, rice and soups to imbue them with its tang. The people of Reggio Emilia and Parma (provinces of Emilia-Romagna where true Parmesan cheese, called *Parmigiano Reggiano*, is made) claim it has been made there for 2,000 years. To get the genuine article, look for whole cheese that has a dark golden rind stamped with the words "Parmigiano Reggiano."

Sardinian-Style Spaghetti With Pork & Mushrooms

Sardegna

SPAGHETTI CON MAIALE ALLA SARDEGNA

MAKES 4 TO 6 SERVINGS

½ green bell pepper, cut into strips
½ red bell pepper, cut into strips
1 medium onion, cut into 8 wedges
2 tablespoons olive oil
1 (1½-pound) pork tenderloin, cut into ½-inch cubes
   Salt and pepper
2 cloves garlic, chopped
2 (26-ounce) jars Classico₍₎ di Sicilia (Mushrooms & Ripe
   Olives) Pasta Sauce
¼ cup dry white vermouth or wine
½ teaspoon dried thyme leaves
1 (1-pound) package Classico₍₎ Spaghetti, cooked as package
   directs and drained

In large skillet, over medium-high heat, cook and stir peppers and onion in oil until tender-crisp; remove vegetables from skillet. Season pork lightly with salt and pepper. In same skillet, cook and stir pork and garlic until browned. Reduce heat; add pasta sauce, vermouth and thyme. Simmer, covered, until pork is tender, about 20 minutes, stirring occasionally. Add vegetables; heat through. Serve over hot cooked spaghetti. Refrigerate leftovers.

Sardegna is renowned for its amazing rainbow of breads—most notably its thin, flat, crisp breads. The thinnest and crispiest of them all is called *fogli di musica*, literally "sheet music." If there doesn't happen to be a Sardegnan bakery around the corner, serve this Sardegnan-style spaghetti dish with a crisp, cracker-style flat bread such as lavosh.

Gnocchi with Link Sausage & Fennel

GNOCCHI ABRUZZESE

MAKES 6 TO 8 SERVINGS

1	**pound Italian sausage links, sliced into 1-inch pieces**
2	**cloves garlic, chopped**
2	**(26-ounce) jars Classico® d'Abruzzi (Italian Sausage & Fennel) Pasta Sauce**
¼	**to ½ teaspoon dried red pepper flakes**
1	**(1-pound) package Classico® Gnocchi, cooked as package directs and drained**
½	**cup freshly shredded Parmesan cheese**

In saucepan, over medium heat, brown sausage; pour off fat. Add garlic; cook and stir until tender. Add pasta sauce and red pepper flakes. Bring to a boil; reduce heat. Simmer, covered, 15 minutes, stirring occasionally. Serve over hot cooked gnocchi. Sprinkle with Parmesan cheese; garnish with fresh dill. Refrigerate leftovers.

Italian Bread

Combine 2 cups *all-purpose flour*, 2 packages *active dry yeast* and 1½ teaspoons *salt*. Add 2 cups *warm water* (120° to 130°). Beat 30 seconds, scraping bowl. Beat on high speed 3 minutes. Measure 4 cups *flour* into a bowl; stir as much flour into dough as you can. Knead in enough remaining flour to make a stiff dough that is smooth and elastic (8 to 10 minutes). Shape into a ball. Place in a large greased bowl; turn once. Cover; let rise in warm place until doubled (1 to 1½ hours). Punch down. Divide in half. Cover; let rest 10 minutes. Grease 2 baking sheets; sprinkle with *cornmeal*. Roll into 15x12-inch rectangles. Roll up from long sides; seal well. Taper ends. Place seam sides down on baking sheets. Beat 1 *egg white* with 1 tablespoon *water*; brush some on dough. Cover; let rise until *nearly* doubled (45 minutes). Make cuts ¼ inch deep across tops. Preheat oven to 375°. Bake 15 minutes. Brush with egg white mixture. Bake 10 minutes or until golden. Makes 2 loaves.

Start a dinner of these gnocchi with an appetizer of savory herbed mushrooms. Choose large, flat mushrooms such as portobellos. Trim the stems down almost to the caps. Cover caps with a mixture of finely chopped fresh Italian parsley and minced garlic. Lightly season with salt and dried red pepper flakes. Drizzle about a teaspoon of olive oil over each mushroom, and then broil or grill them about 10 minutes. Serve immediately.

Braised Beef with Red Wine Trieste

Friuli-Venezia Giulia

MANZO ALLA TRIESTE

MAKES 6 TO 8 SERVINGS

1 (2-pound) beef sirloin tip, bottom round or chuck roast
   Salt and pepper
4 slices bacon
1 pound yellow onions, sliced (about 3½ cups)
1 cup dry red wine
1 (26-ounce) jar Classico® di Milano (Garden Zucchini & Parmesan) Pasta Sauce
2 bay leaves
2 tablespoons chopped fresh or 1 teaspoon dried rosemary leaves
2 tablespoons chopped fresh or 1 teaspoon dried marjoram leaves
1 tablespoon paprika
1 (1-pound) package Classico® Gnocchi, cooked as package directs and drained

Season roast lightly with salt and pepper. In Dutch oven, over medium heat, cook bacon until crisp. Remove from Dutch oven. Drain on paper towels and crumble; set aside. In *2 tablespoons* drippings, brown roast; remove from Dutch oven. Add onions; cook and stir over medium-high heat until tender. Add wine; boil 10 minutes, stirring occasionally. Stir in pasta sauce, bay leaves, rosemary, marjoram and paprika; mix well. Add roast. Bring to a boil; reduce heat and simmer, covered, until meat is tender, about 1½ hours. Remove bay leaves. Serve sliced meat and sauce with hot cooked gnocchi; garnish with bacon. Refrigerate leftovers.

Serve this hearty beef dish with a full-flavored red wine, such as a Bardolino or Valpolicella, that is produced in the area of the *Tre Venezie*, or "three Venices." For an authentic touch, decant it and serve as they do in the modest restaurants of Trieste: in a rustic pitcher.

Italian Veal Stew With Rosemary

SPEZZATINO DI VITELLO AL ABRUZZI

MAKES 6 SERVINGS

1½   **pounds boneless veal cubes for stew**
    Salt and pepper
    Flour
  2   **to 3 tablespoons olive oil**
¼   **cup chopped shallots**
  2   **cloves garlic, finely chopped**
  1   **(26-ounce) jar Classico® d'Abruzzi (Italian Sausage & Fennel)**
    Pasta Sauce
¼   **cup dry Marsala wine**
  1   **teaspoon dried rosemary leaves, crumbled**
  1   **(1-pound) package Classico® Farfalle, cooked as package**
    directs and drained

Season veal lightly with salt and pepper; coat with flour. In large saucepan, over medium heat, brown meat in oil; remove from pan. Add shallots and garlic; cook and stir until shallots are tender. Add veal, pasta sauce, wine and rosemary; mix well. Bring to a boil; reduce heat and simmer, covered, until veal is tender, about 40 minutes, stirring occasionally. Serve over hot cooked farfalle. Refrigerate leftovers.

Sicilia's greatest gift to the world of wine, Marsala, was created by sheer serendipity. During the 17th century, when great quantities of Sicilian wine were being shipped to England, one part alcohol was added to 50 parts wine to fortify it for the long voyage. Connoisseurs took a great liking to the rich, smooth taste of the resultant wine. It wasn't until nearly a century later, however, that an Englishman named John Woodhouse moved to Marsala and began to make its namesake wine in earnest.

Veal Cutlets Trentino With Fettuccine

Trentino-Alto Adige

COTOLETTI DI VITELLO CON FETTUCCINE

MAKES 4 TO 6 SERVINGS

- **2 eggs**
- **2 tablespoons water**
- **½ teaspoon salt**
- **4 to 6 veal cutlets, each cut in half (1 to 1½ pounds total)**
- **1½ cups dry bread crumbs**
- **⅓ cup butter or margarine**
- **3 tablespoons olive oil**
- **¾ cup chopped onion**
- **2 cloves garlic, chopped**
- **2 (26-ounce) jars Classico® di Firenze (Florentine Spinach & Cheese) Pasta Sauce**
- **1 (1-pound) package Classico® Fettuccine, cooked as package directs and drained**

In bowl, beat eggs, water and salt. Dip veal in egg mixture, then in bread crumbs. In large skillet, over medium heat, melt butter with *2 tablespoons* oil. Brown veal on both sides; drain. In medium saucepan, cook onion and garlic in remaining *1 tablespoon* oil until tender. Add pasta sauce; heat through. Place hot cooked fettuccine on serving plate; top with sauce, then veal and additional sauce, if desired. Refrigerate leftovers.

The area of Trentino in northeastern Italy is decidedly Tyrolean in its art, architecture and food—including its fondness for Austrian-style pastries, strudels, sauerkraut and white wines. Serve the tender and light veal dish at left with a light red or white wine and follow it with dessert featuring rich pastries and fresh fruit.

The South: Sun, Sea And Spice

The South of Italy, from Lazio, Molise and down—and including the island of Sicilia—is a sun-and-sea-kissed place that mirrors its climate in its cuisine. The azure-blue sea surrounding Southern Italy's coastline yields a plentitude of seafood. Pastas of all shapes, embellished with sauces made from vegetables cultivated in the South's rich volcanic soil, are often touched with another kind of fire—the robust taste of red-hot chili peppers.

Clockwise from left: Neapolitan Mozzarella "Pockets" (see recipe, page 55), Capellini with Sicilian Fisherman's Sauce (see recipe, page 78) and Vegetable Garden Pizza (see recipe, page 59).

Tiny green capers— the flower buds of the caper bush— pack intense flavor in very little space. Italian capers are the best in the world—particularly those grown on the island of Pantelleria off the Sicilian coast, where volcanic soil and an arid climate provide ideal conditions. Caper buds are pickled in vinegar and salt. Their pungent flavor is primarily used to flavor sauces for pastas and meats.

Black Olive Pâté *Sicilia*

PÂTÉ D'OLIVE

MAKES 12 SERVINGS

1 **(1-pound) package Classico® Farfalle, cooked as package directs and drained**
  Cooking oil for frying
  Freshly grated Parmesan cheese
2 **cups cured ripe Italian olives, pitted and coarsely chopped (about ½ pound)**
2 **tablespoons olive oil**
1 **tablespoon capers, drained and rinsed**
4 **anchovy fillets, rinsed and coarsely chopped**
2 **cloves garlic, chopped**
1 **teaspoon chopped fresh thyme leaves or ½ teaspoon dried Italian seasoning**

Pat farfalle dry with paper towels. Fry in 1½ inches hot oil until lightly browned on both sides. Drain on paper towels and immediately sprinkle with Parmesan cheese. Store, covered, at room temperature. In food processor or blender, combine olives, olive oil, capers, anchovies, garlic and thyme; blend until smooth. (Mixture should be coarse, but spreadable.) Serve along with fried pasta. Store pâté, tightly covered, in the refrigerator for 3 to 4 weeks (a thin layer of olive oil on top will help preserve the rich flavor).

Neapolitan Mozzarella "Pockets" *Campania*

TASCHE DI MOZZARELLA NAPOLETANA

MAKES 16 SERVINGS

Olive oil

4 **(½-pound) packages unsliced mozzarella cheese,** *each* **cut crosswise into 4 equal portions**

8 **cured ripe Italian or Greek olives, pitted and cut into quarters**

8 **small anchovy fillets,** *each* **cut in half**

1 **(26-ounce) jar Classico® di Napoli (Tomato & Basil) Pasta Sauce**

Toasted or freshly sliced Italian bread

Preheat oven to 400°. Brush two 9-inch pie plates with olive oil. With small sharp knife, cut a small pocket in a flat side of *each* mozzarella piece. Stuff *each* pocket with 2 olive pieces and 1 anchovy piece. Place in prepared pie plates. Spoon pasta sauce over cheese pieces. Bake until cheese *begins* to melt, about 8 minutes. Serve immediately with toast. Refrigerate leftovers.

Pictured on pages 52–53.

The balmy climate of Naples has encouraged a Neapolitan love for the *al fresco* life. The streets of Naples pulse with musicians, magicians, clowns of all kinds and, of course, the food vendors. Naples has been famed for its street food since the 19th century when spaghetti, covered in hot tomato sauce and freshly grated Parmesan cheese, was the favorite street "snack." Today, pizza is the al fresco food of choice, hand-held and folded in half to keep the topping intact.

Capellini Fritters *Calabria*

CAPELLINI FRITTI

MAKES 12 TO 14 FRITTERS

½ **(1-pound) package Classico® Capellini, broken into fourths, cooked as package directs and drained**

3 **eggs**

¼ **cup freshly grated pecorino Romano or Parmesan cheese**

½ **teaspoon freshly ground black pepper**
 Olive oil
 Classico® Pasta Sauce, any flavor, heated

In medium bowl, beat eggs with Romano cheese and pepper; stir in cooked capellini. In nonstick skillet, over medium heat, heat 2 *tablespoons* oil. Drop ¼ *cup* capellini mixture into skillet for each fritter; press down slightly. Cook until lightly browned on both sides. Drain on paper towels. Repeat, adding more oil as needed. Serve warm with pasta sauce. Refrigerate leftovers.

These pasta fritters would make an excellent lunch or light dinner served with a refreshing salad of fennel and oranges. Simply clean and julienne a fennel bulb, peel and section two oranges and toss with extra-virgin olive oil. Season to taste with salt and freshly ground black pepper. Garnish each serving with a few toasted pine nuts.

Sautéed Eggplant, Potato & Peppers *Basilicata*
MELANZANE E PATATE BASILICATA
MAKES 6 TO 8 SERVINGS

2   medium eggplants, cut into 1-inch cubes
2   pounds baking potatoes, pared and cut into 1-inch cubes
5   tablespoons olive oil
1   large green bell pepper, coarsely chopped
6   cloves garlic, coarsely chopped
1   (26-ounce) jar Classico® di Roma Arrabbiata (Spicy Red Pepper) Pasta Sauce
    Chopped fresh Italian parsley

In large bowl, combine eggplant and potatoes; mix well. In large nonstick skillet, over medium-high heat, cook and stir *half* the eggplant mixture in *2 tablespoons* oil until lightly browned and potatoes are tender. Remove from skillet. Repeat with remaining eggplant mixture and *2 tablespoons* oil. In Dutch oven, over medium heat, cook pepper and garlic in remaining *1 tablespoon* oil until tender. Stir in pasta sauce and cooked eggplant mixture. Bring to a boil; reduce heat and simmer 10 minutes. Transfer eggplant mixture to a serving bowl; top with parsley. Refrigerate leftovers.

Roasting garlic gives it a sweet, caramelized flavor and quiets its roar. To roast garlic, cut about ¼ inch off the pointed end of the bulb to expose the cloves. If you don't have a garlic baker, place the bulb on a piece of aluminum foil large enough to cover it, drizzle with some extra-virgin olive oil and sprinkle with salt and some fresh herbs such as rosemary or thyme. Wrap and roast it in a 350° oven about 45 minutes or until cloves are soft and golden. Serve garlic spread on bread with cheese and roasted peppers.

Vegetable Garden Pizza *Campania*

PIZZA GIARDINIERA

MAKES TWO 12-INCH PIZZAS

2 (12-inch) Italian bread shells or Homemade Pizza Crusts
1 (26-ounce) jar Classico® di Capri (Sun-Dried Tomato) or
   di Napoli (Tomato & Basil) Pasta Sauce
   Pizza toppings: coarsely chopped or sliced red, green or
   yellow bell peppers; sliced ripe olives; chopped or sliced
   sun-dried tomatoes; sliced fresh mushrooms; sliced
   pepperoni; chopped fresh basil or oregano leaves
2 cups (½ pound) shredded mozzarella cheese

Preheat oven to 450°. Top *each* bread shell with pasta sauce, desired toppings and mozzarella cheese. Bake 10 to 12 minutes or until hot and bubbly. Let stand 5 minutes. Refrigerate leftovers.

Homemade Pizza Crusts: In medium bowl, dissolve 2 tablespoons *active dry yeast* in 1 cup warm *water* (105°). Stir in 2 cups *all-purpose flour* to make a sponge. Cover; let rise in a warm place 45 minutes. In large bowl, combine 2 additional cups *flour* and 1 teaspoon *salt*; add risen sponge and mix well. Turn out on a lightly floured surface and knead until smooth and silky, about 5 minutes, adding additional *flour*, if necessary. Place dough in large lightly oiled bowl. Brush top and side of dough lightly with *oil*. Cover; let rise in a warm place until nearly doubled, about 2 hours. Punch down dough and divide in half. Roll each half into a 12-inch circle. Place on pizza pans; top and bake as directed above.

Pictured on pages 52–53.

The pizza of Naples has a distinctively crisp texture and slightly wood-smoked flavor—imparted by the centuries-old tradition of baking it at a very high heat in a wood-fired clay or brick oven. To get a similar effect, bake a pizza on a baking stone or place some terra-cotta tiles on the lower shelf of your oven. Bake the pizza on the top shelf, and, at the beginning of the baking time, toss a couple of ice cubes on the oven floor. The steam will crisp the crust.

Antipasto Salad Amalfi *Campania*
INSALATA ANTIPASTI D'AMALFI
MAKES 10 TO 12 SERVINGS

- 1 (1-pound) package Classico® Farfalle, cooked as package directs and drained
- 2 cups chopped mixed fresh vegetables (carrots, celery, green bell pepper, cauliflowerets)
- 1 (15- or 16-ounce) can garbanzo beans or chick peas, drained
- 2 (9-ounce) packages frozen artichoke hearts, thawed
- ½ cup sliced green onions
- ½ cup chopped fresh Italian parsley
- ¼ cup sliced ripe olives
- 1½ cups (½ of a 26-ounce jar) Classico® di Napoli (Tomato & Basil) or di Sorrento (Onion & Garlic) Pasta Sauce
- ½ cup olive oil
- ½ cup red wine vinegar
- 1 teaspoon Dijon-style mustard
- 1 clove garlic, finely chopped
- 3 Italian plum tomatoes, chopped (about 1½ cups)
- ½ pound provolone or mozzarella cheese, cut into cubes
- 4 to 8 ounces salami, cut into thin strips

In large bowl, combine cooked farfalle, mixed fresh vegetables, garbanzo beans, artichoke hearts, green onions, parsley and olives; mix well. In small bowl, combine pasta sauce, oil, vinegar, mustard and garlic; stir into pasta mixture. Cover; chill thoroughly. To serve, arrange farfalle mixture on serving platter; top with tomatoes, provolone cheese and salami. Refrigerate leftovers.

The classic languid Italian meal consists of five to six courses: an *antipasto* of such foods as thinly sliced meats, light fresh seafood, cheeses, olives or vegetables; a *primo piatto*, or first course, of pasta, rice or polenta; a *secondo piatto* of meat or fish; *insalata*, or salad; and, finally, fresh fruit and cheese followed by a sweet. These days, even Italians—who are traditionalists about food—aren't eating all of the courses, but are turning the *primo piatto* into the main course.

Vegetable Market Capellini

CAPELLINI ALLA MERCATO

MAKES 6 TO 8 SERVINGS

1	cup sliced fresh mushrooms
¾	cup chopped onion
2	cloves garlic, chopped
2	tablespoons olive oil
2	(26-ounce) jars Classico® di Capri (Sun-Dried Tomato) Pasta Sauce
1½	teaspoons dried Italian seasoning
1	(6-ounce) jar artichoke hearts marinated in olive oil, drained and chopped
1½	cups fresh small broccoli flowerets
1½	cups fresh small cauliflowerets
½	cup coarsely chopped yellow bell pepper
1	(1-pound) package Classico® Capellini, cooked as package directs and drained
	Freshly grated Parmesan cheese

In large saucepan, over medium heat, cook and stir mushrooms, onion and garlic in oil until vegetables are tender. Add pasta sauce and Italian seasoning. Simmer, covered, 15 minutes. Add artichoke hearts, broccoli, cauliflowerets and pepper. Simmer, covered, 20 minutes longer or until vegetables are tender. Serve over hot cooked capellini topped with Parmesan cheese. Refrigerate leftovers.

There are grocery stores in Italy, called *alimentari,* but they are mainly for the purchase of dry goods. The bustling Italian markets that fill the square of even the smallest Italian village are where the real food is bought. The region and the season determine the precise offerings of the market. A constant element, however, is the array of beautiful, bright fruits and vegetables that grace even the simplest Italian meal.

Spaghetti Carbonara

SPAGHETTI CARBONARA ALLA ROMA
MAKES 6 TO 8 SERVINGS

  3 **eggs**
 ¼ **cup freshly grated Parmesan cheese**
 ¼ **cup freshly grated pecorino Romano cheese**
  2 **tablespoons chopped fresh chives**
 ½ **teaspoon freshly ground black pepper**
 ½ **pound sliced bacon**
  1 **tablespoon olive oil or butter**
  4 **cloves garlic, chopped**
  2 **tablespoons chopped fresh or 1 teaspoon dried basil leaves**
  1 **(1-pound) package Classico® Spaghetti, cooked as package directs and drained**
    Freshly grated Parmesan cheese

In medium bowl, beat together eggs, the ¼ *cup* Parmesan cheese, Romano cheese, chives and pepper; set aside. In Dutch oven, cook bacon in oil until crisp; drain bacon on paper towels and crumble. Add garlic and basil to drippings; cook and stir over low heat until garlic is tender. Stir in hot cooked spaghetti, then egg mixture. Toss quickly until well blended and egg mixture is set. Remove from heat; top with crumbled bacon. Serve immediately topped with *additional* Parmesan cheese. Refrigerate leftovers.

Tip: For a creamier dish, beat 1 cup (½ pint) *half-and-half* with egg mixture. Proceed as directed.

The well-equipped Italian kitchen requires a few simple but essential items. A proper *batteria di cucina* includes an array of pots, both small and large; casseroles and pans for baking lasagna; a *mezzaluna*, a half-moon-shape knife for chopping vegetables; a large slotted spoon for retrieving gnocchi and pasta; a large grater for fresh Parmesan cheese and a small one for lemon zest and nutmeg; and a very large strainer—with feet—for draining cooked pasta in the sink.

Fusilli with Oranges, Red Onion & Black Pepper Butter

FUSILLI CON ARANCIA CALABRESE

MAKES 6 TO 8 SERVINGS

1 (1-pound) package Classico® Fusilli, cooked as package directs and drained
Black Pepper Butter
1 small red onion, sliced and separated into rings
1 tablespoon butter or margarine
8 navel oranges, peeled and sectioned
½ to ¾ cup coarsely chopped walnuts, toasted
½ cup freshly grated pecorino Romano or Parmesan cheese

Prepare Black Pepper Butter; set aside. In large skillet, over medium heat, cook onion in the *1 tablespoon* butter until tender. Add Black Pepper Butter and orange sections; heat until butter is melted. In large pasta bowl, pour orange mixture over hot cooked fusilli; mix gently. Sprinkle with walnuts and Romano cheese. Refrigerate leftovers.

Black Pepper Butter: In small saucepan, over medium-high heat, combine ½ cup *dry white wine* and 2 tablespoons chopped *shallots*. Boil 2 minutes. Remove from heat; stir in 1 cup *butter or margarine*, softened, and 2 tablespoons *freshly ground black pepper*.

Southern Italy's citrus groves have cultivated a love of fruit among its people. The essence of citrus finds its way into so many southern Italian foods: *Zuccherene*—big, soft, lemony sugar cookies; homemade *marmalata,* or marmalade; Italian lemon ice; and *cassata,* a Sicilian cake made with candied orange peel, to name just a few. Blood oranges, with their juicy, red pulp, are even made into a sweet dessert wine for dipping anise-flavored biscotti.

A delicious legacy of Arab rule in Sicily is *gelato*, the rich frozen-custard cousin of ice cream. The Sicilians first learned from the Arabs to make *sorbetti*, frozen drinks of milk and honey. Then, in the 17th century, a Sicilian invented a machine that homogenized egg custard, fruit juices, sugar and ice. Finally, in the 19th century, the process of making gelato with egg yolks and cream was perfected in Sicilia—and the whole world rejoiced.

Spaghetti with Black Olive Sauce

SPAGHETTI CON OLIVE

MAKES 4 SERVINGS

½	**cup finely chopped onion**
1	**tablespoon butter or margarine**
½	**cup half-and-half**
1	**teaspoon freshly ground black pepper**
1	**teaspoon purchased black olive pâté***
1	**cup freshly grated pecorino Romano cheese**
½	**(1-pound) package Classico® Spaghetti, cooked as package directs and drained**
	Chopped fresh Italian parsley

In small saucepan, over medium heat, cook onion in butter until tender. Add half-and-half, pepper and olive pâté. Bring to a boil; boil 1 minute. Reduce heat to low; gradually blend in Romano cheese. Heat through. Serve over hot cooked spaghetti, and garnish with parsley. Refrigerate leftovers.

***Note:** Look for black olive pâté in the olive or condiment section of your supermarket or at Italian specialty stores.

Custard Cream Gelato

In large saucepan, combine 3 cups *milk*, 1⅓ cups *sugar* and 12 beaten *egg yolks*. Cook and stir over medium heat until mixture just begins to coat a metal spoon. Remove from heat; stir in 3 cups *milk* and 1 tablespoon grated *lemon or orange rind*. Cover surface with plastic wrap. Chill thoroughly. Freeze in 4- or 5-quart ice cream freezer according to manufacturer's directions. Store leftovers in freezer. Makes about 2½ quarts.

Baked Rigatoni & Eggplant Neapolitan

Campania

Rigatoni e Melanzane Napolitana

MAKES 6 TO 8 SERVINGS

1   medium eggplant, pared and sliced into ¼-inch slices
    Olive oil
½   (1-pound) package Classico® Rigatoni, cooked as package
    directs and drained
1   (26-ounce) jar Classico® di Salerno (Sweet Peppers &
    Onions) Pasta Sauce
2   cups (½ pound) shredded mozzarella cheese
⅓   cup freshly grated pecorino Romano or Parmesan cheese

Preheat oven to 425°. In large skillet, cook eggplant, a few slices at a time, in oil until well browned. Drain on paper towels; keep warm. Reserving *1 cup* pasta sauce, combine remaining sauce with cooked rigatoni. In 2-quart shallow baking dish, layer *half* the rigatoni mixture, *¾ cup* mozzarella cheese, *half* the eggplant and *2 tablespoons* Romano cheese; repeat. Top with reserved *1 cup* pasta sauce and remaining cheeses. Bake, uncovered, 15 minutes or until hot and bubbly. Refrigerate leftovers.

Amaretto Chocolate Mousse

In saucepan, combine ⅓ cup *sugar*, 2 tablespoons *flour* and 2 tablespoons *unsweetened cocoa*. Add ¾ cup *milk*. Cook and stir until thickened; cook and stir 2 minutes longer. Stir hot mixture into 2 *egg yolks*; return to saucepan. Cook and stir until bubbly; cook and stir 2 minutes longer. Remove from heat; stir in 1 tablespoon *butter or margarine* and 1 tablespoon *amaretto*. Cover surface with plastic wrap; chill 1 to 2 hours or until cooled but not set. Whip ¾ cup *whipping cream* until soft peaks form. Fold about *one-fourth* whipped cream into chocolate mixture; fold in remaining cream. Cover; chill. Refrigerate leftovers. Serves 4.

Southern Italians have a penchant for candied fruit. To add a particularly Neapolitan touch to plain mousse, pierce several candied cherries with a fork and soak them in rum overnight. Just before serving the mousse, garnish each serving with a few soaked cherries and top with a small spoonful or two of the soaking liquid.

Baked Rigatoni with Broccoli & Cheese *Sicilia*

RIGATONI CON BROCCOLI AL FORNO

MAKES 6 TO 8 SERVINGS

½	**(1-pound) package Classico® Rigatoni, cooked as package directs and drained**
6	**cups small fresh broccoli flowerets, steamed**
1	**red bell pepper, roasted, peeled, seeded and coarsely chopped**
1	**pound mozzarella cheese**
¾	**cup chopped onion**
⅓	**cup olive oil**
1	**(26-ounce) jar Classico® di Sorrento (Onion & Garlic) Pasta Sauce**
½	**teaspoon freshly ground black pepper**
1	**(3½-ounce) can medium pitted whole ripe olives, drained and halved**
¼	**cup freshly grated pecorino Romano cheese**

Preheat oven to 375°. Shred *¼ pound* mozzarella cheese; cut remaining *¾ pound* mozzarella cheese into ½-inch cubes. Set aside. In Dutch oven, over medium-high heat, cook onion in oil until tender. Stir in pasta sauce and black pepper; heat through. Remove from heat; add the *cubed* mozzarella cheese, cooked rigatoni, broccoli, roasted red pepper, olives and Romano cheese; mix well. Turn into greased 13x9-inch baking dish. Bake, tightly covered, until hot and bubbly, about 40 minutes. Uncover; top with the *shredded* mozzarella cheese. Bake 5 minutes longer. Refrigerate leftovers.

The phrase *al forno* simply means "from the oven." A practical and delightful way to cook, al forno usually refers to any one of the possible combinations of meat, poultry or seafood, vegetables, pasta, sauce and cheeses dreamed up by the cook (or yielded by the pantry), layered into a casserole, and baked until hot and bubbly.

Penne with Chicken & Artichokes

PENNE E POLLO CON CARCIOFI
MAKES 6 TO 8 SERVINGS

Lazio

½ pound sliced fresh mushrooms
½ cup chopped green onions
4 cloves garlic, chopped
½ cup dry red wine
1 to 1½ pounds skinned, boneless chicken breast halves, cut
   into 1-inch cubes
3 tablespoons chopped fresh or 1 teaspoon dried basil leaves
2 tablespoons olive oil
2 (26-ounce) jars Classico® di Capri (Sun-Dried Tomato)
   Pasta Sauce
1 (9-ounce) package frozen artichoke hearts, thawed
   and sliced
1 cup (½ pint) whipping cream
1 (1-pound) package Classico® Penne Rigate, cooked as
   package directs and drained

In Dutch oven, over medium heat, cook mushrooms, green onions
and garlic in wine until mushrooms are tender, about 3 minutes.
Remove mixture from Dutch oven; set aside. In same Dutch oven,
over medium-high heat, brown chicken with basil in oil. Stir in pasta
sauce, artichokes and mushroom mixture. Bring to a boil; reduce heat
and simmer, covered, 15 minutes, stirring occasionally. Stir in cream.
Heat through. Serve over hot cooked penne. Refrigerate leftovers.

Cannoli

Combine 2 cups *ricotta cheese*, ¼ cup *granulated sugar* and
1 teaspoon *vanilla extract*. Stir until smooth. Fold in ¼ cup *mini
semisweet chocolate chips*. Cover; chill. With a pastry bag fitted with
a large tip, pipe mixture into 12 *purchased cannoli cones*. Sift
confectioners' sugar atop. Serves 12.

efore
serving
sweet, creamy
cannoli for dessert,
balance the
vegetable-rich main
course on this page
with a traditional
fruit course. If
they're available, a
refreshing choice
would be the
melons and juicy
blood oranges that
are so plentiful in
southern Italy.

Chicken with Summer Vegetables Campania

 Campania

POLLO DELL'ESTATE

MAKES 6 TO 8 SERVINGS

1   pound skinned, boneless chicken breast halves,
    cut into strips
    Salt and pepper
    Flour
¼   cup olive oil
1   cup chopped onion
2   cloves garlic, chopped
2   (26-ounce) jars Classico® di Napoli (Tomato & Basil) or
    di Capri (Sun-Dried Tomato) Pasta Sauce
2   tablespoons chopped fresh or 1 teaspoon dried
    oregano leaves
3   cups cubed eggplant
2   medium yellow squash, sliced and halved
2   medium zucchini, sliced and halved
1   medium green bell pepper, cut into strips
1   (1-pound) package Classico® Fusilli, cooked as package
    directs and drained
    Freshly shredded Parmesan cheese

Season chicken lightly with salt and pepper; coat with flour. In large saucepan, over medium-high heat, brown chicken in oil. Remove chicken from pan. In same saucepan, cook and stir onion and garlic until tender. Add chicken, pasta sauce and oregano. Simmer, covered, 20 minutes. Add eggplant, squash, zucchini and bell pepper. Simmer, covered, 15 minutes longer. Serve over hot cooked fusilli with Parmesan cheese. Refrigerate leftovers.

Pictured on the cover.

Southern sun-dried tomatoes are used throughout Italy today for their intense flavor. To make them yourself, wash and core ripe tomatoes, then slice ⅛ inch thick. Lay on baking sheets. Dry in 120° oven for 18 to 24 hours, turning slices and rotating sheets twice. For extra flavor, pour some boiling water over the tomatoes to rehydrate. Pack in a clean jar with olive oil. Store in a cool place, and use within a few months. Be sure tomatoes are covered with oil so they don't mold.

Turkey, Sweet Pepper & Mozzarella Rolls

Basilicata

BRACIOLE DI DINDO IMBOTTITI

MAKES 6 SERVINGS

2   small green, red or yellow bell peppers, cut into strips
1   clove garlic, finely chopped
3   tablespoons olive oil
6   (4-ounce) fresh turkey breast slices
    Salt and pepper
3   ounces sliced mozzarella cheese, cut into 12 strips
1   (26-ounce) jar Classico® di Salerno (Sweet Peppers & Onions) Pasta Sauce
½   (1-pound) package Classico® Linguine, cooked as package directs and drained

In large skillet, cook pepper strips and garlic in *2 tablespoons* oil until tender; remove from pan. Pound *each* turkey slice; season lightly with salt and pepper. On *each* turkey slice, place 2 or 3 pepper strips and 2 cheese strips. Roll tightly and secure with wooden picks. In same skillet, heat remaining *1 tablespoon* oil. Over medium-high heat, brown turkey rolls. Add pasta sauce and remaining peppers. Reduce heat; simmer, covered, until turkey is no longer pink, about 10 minutes. Remove picks; serve over hot cooked linguine. Refrigerate leftovers.

A *batti-carne,* a meat pounder that vaguely resembles a discus with a handle, is favored in most Italian kitchens over a mallet-shaped meat tenderizer. It is used to flatten and tenderize meats such as veal for *scaloppine,* certain cuts of beef and the turkey breasts in this recipe.

Spicy Chicken & Sage Roma

Lazio

POLLO ARRABBIATA ROMA

MAKES 6 TO 8 SERVINGS

1½ pounds skinned, boneless chicken breast halves,
     cut into strips
½   pound sliced fresh mushrooms
¾   cup chopped onion
3   cloves garlic, chopped
⅓   cup olive oil
1   cup dry white vermouth or wine
1   (26-ounce) jar Classico® di Roma Arrabbiata (Spicy Red
     Pepper) Pasta Sauce
2   tablespoons chopped fresh or 1 teaspoon dried sage leaves
1   tablespoon prepared mustard
¼   teaspoon cayenne pepper, optional
½   pound fresh spinach, rinsed, drained and chopped
1   (1-pound) package Classico® Fettuccine, cooked as package
     directs and drained
     Freshly grated Parmesan or pecorino Romano cheese

In Dutch oven, over medium heat, cook chicken, mushrooms, onion
and garlic in oil until chicken is no longer pink. Add vermouth. Bring
to a boil; boil 1 minute. Stir in pasta sauce, sage, mustard and
cayenne pepper, if desired. Simmer, covered, 15 minutes, stirring
occasionally. Stir in spinach; cook, covered, until spinach is tender,
3 minutes. Stir in hot cooked fettuccine. Serve immediately with
Parmesan cheese. Refrigerate leftovers.

talians not only pour wine into glasses, but into their stew pots, too. Wine is used in a myriad of ways in the Italian kitchen: for stewing meats on top of the stove; for creating a meat marinade with olive oil, garlic, lemon juice and spices; and for reducing over low heat with cream to make rich, elegant meat sauces. Drinking wine may sometimes go to the head, but cooking with wine simply imparts a heady flavor to anything it touches.

Shrimp & Scallop Pasta Salad *Puglia*
INSALATA DI FRUTTI DI MARE CON FUSILLI

MAKES 6 TO 8 SERVINGS

1   (1-pound) package Classico® Fusilli, cooked as package directs and drained
1   pound bay scallops
1   pound raw medium shrimp, peeled and deveined
    Salt
½   cup plus 2 tablespoons olive oil
1   medium red bell pepper, cut into strips
1   medium yellow bell pepper, cut into strips
1   medium carrot, cut into thin 1-inch strips
1   medium zucchini, coarsely shredded
½   cup finely chopped shallots
½   cup white wine vinegar
2   tablespoons lemon juice
1   tablespoon *each* finely chopped fresh basil, chervil, chives, Italian parsley and tarragon leaves*
2   cloves garlic, finely chopped

Season scallops and shrimp lightly with salt. In large skillet, over medium-high heat, cook and stir scallops and shrimp in the *2 tablespoons* oil until scallops are opaque and shrimp are pink, about 3 minutes. Remove from heat; drain. In large pasta bowl, combine cooked fusilli, scallops, shrimp, peppers, carrot and zucchini. In small bowl, combine the remaining *½ cup* oil, the shallots, vinegar, lemon juice, herbs and garlic. Add to fusilli mixture; mix well. Cover; chill thoroughly. Refrigerate leftovers.

***Note:** Substitute 2 tablespoons *dried Italian seasoning* for the fresh herbs.

The only accompaniments the light and colorful seafood salad on this page requires are a glass of chilled, fairly dry wine—try a pinot grigio or a white Sicilian wine—and some crusty Italian bread. To do as Italians do, serve the bread with a small dish of extra-virgin olive oil embellished with freshly ground black pepper, a couple of capers and a few fresh gratings of Parmesan cheese.

Spicy Sicilian Seafood Stew

Sicilia

ZUPPA DI FRUTTI DI MARE SICILIANA

MAKES 8 SERVINGS

1   **pound carrots, cut into ½-inch slices and cooked**
3   **cloves garlic, chopped**
½   **cup olive oil**
⅓   **cup dry white vermouth or wine**
1   **(26-ounce) jar Classico® di Sicilia (Mushrooms & Ripe Olives) Pasta Sauce**
1   **(9-ounce) package frozen artichoke hearts, thawed**
1½ **teaspoons ground turmeric**
¾   **teaspoon salt**
½   **teaspoon cayenne pepper**
1   **pound sea scallops**
1   **pound raw medium shrimp, peeled, leaving tails on, if desired, and deveined**
2   **pounds small baking potatoes, baked or boiled until tender and sliced**

In large kettle, over medium-high heat, cook and stir carrots and garlic in *¼ cup* oil until carrots begin to brown. Add vermouth; bring to a boil. Boil 3 minutes. Stir in pasta sauce, artichokes, *1 teaspoon* turmeric, *½ teaspoon* salt and *¼ teaspoon* cayenne pepper. Bring to a boil; reduce heat and simmer, covered, 15 minutes. Stir in scallops and shrimp; simmer, covered, until scallops are opaque and shrimp are pink, about 3 minutes. In small bowl, combine remaining *½ teaspoon* turmeric, *¼ teaspoon* salt and *¼ teaspoon* cayenne pepper. In large skillet, over medium-high heat, brown potatoes in remaining *¼ cup* oil; sprinkle with turmeric mixture. Serve potatoes with the stew. Refrigerate leftovers.

The spice turmeric, used in the seafood stew at left, is a gastronomic signpost that Sicilia is a mere 90 miles from the coast of north Africa. However, it is the influence of the Arabs, who invaded and conquered Sicilia in the 9th century, that continues to impact the Sicilian palate. Cooks in this region are fond of incorporating into their food such ingredients as couscous, saffron and all things sweet and sour.

Capellini with Sicilian Fisherman's Sauce

CAPELLINI ALLA PESCATORE SICILIANO

MAKES 6 TO 8 SERVINGS

hough this sauce is full of vegetables, Sicilians can never get enough of them. Try accompanying this piquant and slightly sweet sauce with greens—such as escarole (a Sicilian favorite) or spinach—that have been lightly boiled, then sautéed in olive oil with minced garlic. Eat the greens with crusty bread to soak up the delicious sauce.

1	medium eggplant, cut into 1-inch cubes
½	pound small yellow squash, sliced
½	green bell pepper, cut into strips
½	red bell pepper, cut into strips
2	tablespoons chopped fresh or 1 teaspoon dried basil leaves
2	cloves garlic, chopped
⅓	cup olive oil
1	(26-ounce) jar Classico® di Sicilia (Mushrooms & Ripe Olives) Pasta Sauce
¼	cup currants, soaked in warm water and drained
1	tablespoon lemon juice
1	tablespoon finely chopped fresh Italian parsley
1	pound bay scallops
1	(1-pound) package Classico® Capellini, cooked as package directs and drained
	Pine nuts or slivered almonds, toasted

In large skillet, over medium-high heat, cook and stir eggplant, squash, peppers, basil and garlic in oil until tender. Add pasta sauce, currants, lemon juice and parsley; mix well. Bring to a boil; reduce heat and simmer, covered, 10 minutes. Stir in scallops; cook until scallops are opaque, about 3 minutes. Serve over hot cooked capellini. Garnish with pine nuts. Refrigerate leftovers.

Pictured on pages 52–53.

Seacoast Spaghettini with Scampi & Mussels

Campania

SPAGHETTINI CON COZZE E GAMBERI

MAKES 6 TO 8 SERVINGS

- **1 cup chopped onion**
- **3 cloves garlic, finely chopped**
- **2 tablespoons olive oil**
- **2 (26-ounce) jars Classico® di Sorrento (Onion & Garlic) Pasta Sauce**
- **1½ pounds raw medium shrimp, peeled and deveined**
- **1 pound mussels, cleaned and soaked**
- **1 (1-pound) package Classico® Spaghettini, cooked as package directs and drained**

In large kettle, over medium-high heat, cook onion and garlic in oil until tender. Stir in pasta sauce. Bring to a boil; reduce heat and simmer, partially covered, 20 minutes. Add shrimp and mussels; simmer, covered, until mussels open, about 8 minutes. Stir and serve over hot cooked spaghettini. Refrigerate leftovers.

Lemon Sorbetto

Dissolve ½ cup *sugar* in ¼ cup *boiling water*. Add 1 cup *cold water*, ¼ teaspoon finely grated *lemon rind* and ½ cup *lemon juice*. Pour into a 9x5- or 8x4-inch loaf pan. Freeze about 4 hours or until icy; stir. Then freeze for 1 to 3 hours longer or until nearly firm, stirring every 30 minutes. (Or, freeze, without stirring, overnight or until nearly firm.) Place lemon ice mixture in a blender container or food processor bowl. Cover and blend or process until fluffy, stopping once or twice to scrape the side. Spoon lemon ice into small stemmed glasses. Garnish with *lemon slices* and *mint leaves*. Store leftovers in freezer. Makes 6 servings.

When buying live mussels, look for tightly closed shells that are moist and are not cracked or chipped. If any of the shells are open, tap them lightly. If the mussels are alive, the shell should close. Fresh mussels should smell like the sea and not have a strong odor. To clean mussels for cooking, scrub the shells with a stiff brush under cold water. Be sure to remove the beards, visible between the shells, just before cooking, as mussels will die without them.

Spaghettini with Grilled Swordfish

SPAGHETTINI CON SPADA TARANTESE

MAKES 6 TO 8 SERVINGS

1½ **pounds boneless swordfish steaks, cut into 1-inch pieces**
   Salt and pepper
1 **large red bell pepper, cut into 1-inch pieces**
1 **large yellow bell pepper, cut into 1-inch pieces**
¼ **cup olive oil**
½ **cup chopped shallots**
2 **tablespoons butter or margarine**
½ **cup dry white vermouth or wine**
2 **cups (1 pint) half-and-half**
1 **(1-pound) package Classico® Spaghettini, cooked as**
   package directs and drained
¼ **cup chopped fresh chives**

Season swordfish lightly with salt and pepper. Alternately skewer swordfish with red and yellow peppers on skewers.* Brush with oil. Prepare grill. In Dutch oven, over medium heat, cook shallots in butter until tender. Stir in vermouth. Bring to a boil; boil 3 minutes. Add half-and-half; slowly bring to a boil. Simmer 5 minutes. Set aside. Grill swordfish and peppers until fish flakes easily. Heat sauce; add cooked spaghettini and chives. Heat through. To serve, portion hot cooked spaghettini mixture onto serving plates; top *each* portion with swordfish and peppers. Refrigerate leftovers.

***Note:** If using wooden skewers, as shown opposite, soak them in water about 30 minutes before assembling the kabobs.

*U*ntil just recently, swordfish—the fish king of the Southern Italian kitchen—was available only from May to August, when it ventured close to the coasts. So much of this succulent, meaty fish was eaten during those months that every kind of preparation imaginable was devised. The kabob serving style, shown in the photo opposite, reflects the Eastern influence so prevalent in Southern Italian cooking.

Spaghettini with Grilled Swordfish

A simple fruit course is elevated to elegant dessert status with the addition of Marsala. Sprinkle melon balls (preferably cantaloupe or muskmelon) with the fortified Sicilian wine and a few teaspoons of sugar. Stir to coat all of the melon. Let the fruit marinate in the wine and sugar mixture in the refrigerator for a few hours, stirring occasionally, until you're ready to serve. Garnish each serving with fresh mint, if desired.

Sweet & Sour Tuna Steaks *Sicilia*

TONNO AGRODOLCE DI PALERMO

MAKES 8 SERVINGS

- 2 pounds fresh tuna steaks, skin removed
- ¾ cup red wine vinegar
- ½ pound leeks, trimmed, rinsed, chopped and drained
- ¼ cup *plus* 2 tablespoons olive oil
- 1 (26-ounce) jar Classico® di Capri (Sun-Dried Tomato) or di Napoli (Tomato & Basil) Pasta Sauce
- ¼ cup chopped fresh mint leaves
- 2 teaspoons sugar
- ¾ teaspoon salt
- ½ teaspoon freshly ground black pepper
- Flour

Arrange tuna in 13x9-inch baking dish. Pour *½ cup* red wine vinegar over tuna; cover. Marinate 30 minutes, turning twice. In large saucepan, over medium heat, cook and stir the leeks in the *2 tablespoons* oil until tender, about 10 minutes. Stir in pasta sauce, remaining *¼ cup* red wine vinegar, mint, sugar, salt and pepper. Bring to a boil; reduce heat and simmer 5 minutes. Drain tuna; coat with flour. In very large skillet, over medium heat, brown tuna in the remaining *¼ cup* oil until fish flakes. Drain fish on paper towels. Serve immediately with the sauce. Refrigerate leftovers.

Sautéed Carrots

In large skillet, over medium heat, melt 1 tablespoon *butter or margarine*. Add 3 cups thinly sliced *carrots* and 1 clove *garlic*, finely chopped; cook and stir for 5 minutes. Add ½ cup *dry Marsala, dry sherry or chicken broth*; ¼ teaspoon *dried marjoram leaves* and ¼ teaspoon *dried basil leaves*. Cook, uncovered, until carrots are tender-crisp, 5 to 7 minutes, stirring often. Refrigerate leftovers. Makes 4 servings.

Tuna & Mushroom Spaghettini Toss *Calabria*

SPAGHETTINI AL TONNO CALABRESE

MAKES 6 TO 8 SERVINGS

1 ounce dried porcini mushrooms, soaked in water
   30 minutes, drained and coarsely chopped
1 cup chopped fresh Italian parsley
8 cloves garlic, finely chopped
½ teaspoon dried red pepper flakes
½ teaspoon salt
¼ cup olive oil
1 (26-ounce) jar Classico® di Roma Arrabbiata (Spicy Red
   Pepper) Pasta Sauce
1 (12½-ounce) can water-packed tuna, drained
1 (1-pound) package Classico® Spaghettini, cooked as
   package directs and drained

In Dutch oven, over medium heat, cook and stir mushrooms, parsley, garlic, red pepper flakes and salt in oil 5 minutes. Stir in pasta sauce; cook, covered, 10 minutes longer. Add tuna; heat through. Stir in hot cooked spaghettini. Serve immediately. Refrigerate leftovers.

ried mushrooms impart a woodsy flavor and aroma to any dish in which they appear, but they need to be rehydrated first. To rehydrate dried mushrooms, soak them in water 30 minutes, then drain. For even more flavor, try rehydrating them in broth or wine. Let the mushrooms soak about 45 minutes, and don't throw the soaking liquid away. Use it to boost the flavor of a vegetable or cream-based sauce, soup or risotto.

Grocer's Spaghettini *Campania*

SPAGHETTINI ALIMENTARIA

MAKES 6 TO 8 SERVINGS

1   (26-ounce) jar Classico® di Napoli (Tomato & Basil)
      Pasta Sauce
½   pound thinly sliced prosciutto ham, cut into ½-inch pieces
4   ounces hard salami, cut into small strips
1   (1-pound) package Classico® Spaghettini, cooked as
      package directs and drained
½   pound provolone cheese, cut into ½-inch cubes
¼   to ½ teaspoon freshly ground black pepper
1   (6-ounce) jar marinated artichoke hearts, drained

In large saucepan, over medium-high heat, combine pasta sauce, ham and salami. Bring to a boil; reduce heat and simmer, covered, 20 minutes. In large pasta bowl, toss together meat-sauce mixture, hot cooked spaghettini, provolone cheese and pepper. Top with artichokes. Serve immediately. Refrigerate leftovers.

Although the Italian-favored ham, prosciutto, is made in the regions of Emilia-Romagna, Friuli-Venezia Giulia and Toscana—and is eaten with great relish all over Italy—it is the Emilian version that is thought to be superior. It is made from pigs fed on grains, chestnuts and the whey from Parmesan-cheese production. The ham is cured only with sea salt, lard and black pepper in the dry microclimate of Langhirano 20 to 30 miles south of Parma.

Neapolitan Rigatoni & Sausage *Campania*

RIGATONI NAPOLITANA

MAKES 6 TO 8 SERVINGS

1½   pounds link Italian sausage, sliced into 1-inch pieces
1   cup chopped onion
¾   cup chopped green bell pepper
2   (26-ounce) jars Classico® di Capri (Sun-Dried Tomato)
        Pasta Sauce
½   cup freshly grated pecorino Romano or Parmesan cheese
1   (1-pound) package Classico® Rigatoni, cooked as package
        directs and drained
2   tablespoons olive oil

In large saucepan, brown sausage; pour off fat. Add onion and
pepper to saucepan; cook and stir until tender. Add pasta sauce and
Romano cheese. Bring to a boil; reduce heat. Simmer, covered,
15 minutes, stirring occasionally. Toss hot cooked rigatoni with oil.
Serve with sauce. Refrigerate leftovers.

Cauliflower Salad

In a covered medium saucepan, over medium heat, cook 1 medium
head *cauliflower,* broken into flowerets, in a small amount of boiling
water until tender-crisp, 8 to 10 minutes. Drain, transfer to a serving
bowl and let cool. Stir in ½ cup pitted *ripe olives,* halved, and
1 tablespoon *drained capers.* For dressing, in a screw-top jar, combine
¼ cup *olive oil,* ¼ cup *white wine vinegar or cider vinegar,*
½ teaspoon *anchovy paste* (if desired), 1 clove *garlic,* finely chopped,
and ⅛ teaspoon *freshly ground black pepper.* Cover; shake well to
combine. Pour over cauliflower mixture. Cover; chill up to 24 hours,
stirring occasionally. To serve, allow salad to come to room
temperature; top with 1 tablespoon chopped *fresh Italian parsley.*
Refrigerate leftovers. Makes 4 servings.

Neapolitans get as frothy as a cup of *cappuccino* about their love for coffee—and claim to make the best *espresso* in Italy. In the hot summer weather they enjoy *granita,* a sweet coffee-ice sometimes lightly flavored with cocoa. For a similar effect, follow this Neapolitan meal with a dish of refreshing coffee sorbet or ice cream. Top it with a dollop of whipped cream, if you like, and some freshly ground nutmeg.

Braised Pork Chops & Spaghetti Arrabbiata

Spaghetti e Maiale Arrabbiata

Makes 4 servings

1   small green bell pepper, cut into strips
1   small red bell pepper, cut into strips
1   medium onion, cut into 8 wedges
2   cloves garlic, chopped
2   to 3 tablespoons olive oil
4   (¾-inch-thick) center-cut pork chops
     Salt and pepper
     Flour
1   (26-ounce) jar Classico® di Roma Arrabbiata (Spicy Red
     Pepper) Pasta Sauce
¼   cup dry white vermouth or wine
½   teaspoon dried thyme leaves
1   (1-pound) package Classico® Spaghetti, cooked as package
     directs and drained

In large skillet, over medium-high heat, cook peppers, onion and garlic in oil until tender-crisp; remove from skillet. Season pork chops lightly with salt and pepper; coat with flour. In the oil in skillet, brown pork chops. Reduce heat; add pasta sauce, vermouth and thyme. Simmer, covered, 30 minutes or until pork chops are tender, stirring occasionally. Add vegetable mixture; heat through. Serve with hot cooked spaghetti. Refrigerate leftovers.

Like so many foods with a peasant origin, *pinzimonio*—a simple dipping sauce of extra-virgin olive oil, sea salt and freshly ground black pepper—has become chic. In Rome, where it originated, they insist it be made from only the finest olive oil. Now popular as a first course for summer luncheons, it is served with slices of bell peppers, fennel, tomatoes and artichokes.

Savory Eggplant Casserole

Campania

TORTIERE DI MELANZANE E FORMAGGIO

MAKES 8 TO 10 SERVINGS

	Olive oil
8	cups water
2	(¾-pound) eggplants, cut into ¾-inch slices
	Garlic salt
4	ounces bulk Italian sausage, cooked and drained
¾	cup chopped fresh Italian parsley
½	cup unseasoned dry bread crumbs
1	egg
½	teaspoon freshly ground black pepper
¼	teaspoon salt
1	(26-ounce) jar Classico® di Napoli (Tomato & Basil) or di Salerno (Sweet Peppers & Onions) Pasta Sauce
2	ounces thinly sliced provolone cheese (about 5 slices)
1	cup (4 ounces) shredded mozzarella cheese

Preheat oven to 375°. Brush 13x9-inch baking dish with olive oil; set aside. In Dutch oven, over medium-high heat, bring water to a boil; add eggplant slices. Boil 3 minutes. Remove and drain on paper towels. Season eggplant with garlic salt. In medium bowl, combine sausage, parsley, bread crumbs, egg, pepper and salt; mix well. Spread *½ cup* pasta sauce on bottom of prepared baking dish; layer *half* of the eggplant slices, all of the sausage mixture and provolone cheese, *half* of the remaining pasta sauce, then the remaining eggplant and pasta sauce. Bake, covered, 40 minutes or until hot and bubbly. Top with mozzarella cheese. Bake 5 minutes longer. Refrigerate leftovers.

Italians have ingenious ways to use leftover bread: *pappa al pomo-doro*, tomato and bread soup; *panzanella*, bread salad; and *panagrattato*, bread crumbs. In Italy, bread crumbs are sprinkled on gratins, used in stuffings and sauces and are pressed in buttered pans to keep food from sticking. To make bread crumbs, pulverize dry, crustless white bread in a blender or food processor or crush it by hand or with a rolling pin. Store in a tightly sealed plastic bag in the freezer.

Southern Italian Pork Scaloppine
SCALLOPINE DI MAIALE ALL'APULIA
MAKES 8 SERVINGS

1 (2-pound) boneless pork loin, sliced into
¼-inch-thick slices
Salt and pepper
Flour
¼ cup olive oil
¾ cup dry white vermouth or wine
2 tablespoons chopped fresh or 1 teaspoon ground sage
1 (26-ounce) jar Classico® di Sorrento
(Onion & Garlic) Pasta Sauce
¼ cup drained capers

omplement the bright flavors of this Southern Italian meal—with its tongue-nipping hot red peppers and tangy zucchini—by finishing this menu with scoops of cooling, palate-cleansing Lemon Sorbetto (*see recipe, page 79*).

Season pork lightly with salt and pepper. Coat with flour. In large skillet, over medium heat, brown pork slices in oil in batches. Remove from skillet; drain on paper towels. To skillet, add vermouth and sage; bring to a boil. Boil 3 minutes. Add pasta sauce and capers; mix well. Add pork slices; spoon sauce over pork. Bring to a boil; reduce heat. Simmer, covered, 15 minutes. Serve immediately. Refrigerate leftovers.

Neapolitan Zucchini

Cut 3 medium *zucchini* into ½-inch-thick slices. In large skillet, over medium heat, heat 2 tablespoons *olive oil*. Add the zucchini and 2 cloves *garlic*, finely chopped; cook until tender and light golden brown, 3 to 5 minutes. In small bowl, combine ¼ cup *red wine vinegar*, ¼ teaspoon *salt* and ⅛ teaspoon *dried red pepper flakes*. Pour over zucchini in skillet. Remove from heat; let stand until room temperature. Transfer to serving dish. Top with 1 tablespoon chopped *fresh basil leaves*. Refrigerate leftovers. Makes 4 servings.

Beef Steak Sicilian *Sicilia*

BISTECCA SICILIANA

MAKES 8 SERVINGS

3	tablespoons olive oil
1½	cups fresh bread crumbs (3 slices)
2	cloves garlic, finely chopped
1	teaspoon dried oregano leaves
1	(26-ounce) jar Classico® di Sicilia (Mushrooms & Ripe Olives) Pasta Sauce
¼	cup freshly grated pecorino Romano cheese
6	anchovy fillets, finely chopped
8	(4- to 6-ounce) beef tenderloin steaks
	Salt and pepper

In large skillet, heat *1 tablespoon* oil; add crumbs, garlic and oregano. Over medium-high heat, cook and stir until crumbs are golden. In medium bowl, combine crumb mixture, *1¼ cups* pasta sauce, Romano cheese and anchovies; mix well. Season steaks lightly with salt and pepper. In same skillet, heat remaining *2 tablespoons* oil. Over medium-high heat, brown steaks on both sides; reduce heat. Add remaining pasta sauce to skillet with steaks. Top *each* steak with equal portion of crumb mixture. Cook, covered, until heated through and steaks have reached desired doneness, about 5 minutes. Serve immediately. Refrigerate leftovers.

Italian Herbs

Fresh herbs of all kinds are used generously in Italian cooking. Here are a few favorites.

BASIL has a rich, spicy and mildly peppery flavor reminiscent of mint and clove. It is used most often in pasta dishes or served fresh with white beans, tomatoes or cheese drizzled with extra-virgin olive oil.

ROSEMARY is an aromatic herb with a piney taste. Its strong flavor and sturdy sprigs make it ideal for tucking into roasted meats such as lamb and veal. And, it pairs wonderfully with olive oil, garlic and wine.

THYME has a strong, clovelike flavor that complements many foods—most particularly roasted poultry, fish and seafood, slow-cooked soups and stews, sautéed or baked vegetables and tomato-based sauces.

SAGE is a fragrant herb with a slightly lemony, pungent, almost smoky flavor that goes well with roasted meats—especially poultry—and lends Italian pork sausage its familiar savory flavor.

Know Your Pasta

There is a purpose behind pasta shapes. Pick a pasta that is suited to your sauce.

Farfalle
The smooth surface of whimsically shaped bow-tie or butterfly pasta is best suited to delicate olive oil or butter sauces.

Fusilli
Corkscrew pasta, also known as rotelle, captures hearty tomato sauces in its deep ridges.

Rigatoni
The largest tubular pasta with grooves that isn't stuffed, rigatoni should be served with hearty meat sauces.

Gnocchi
Small shapes, like gnocchi and shells, pair well with chunky tomato sauces.

Penne Rigate
A grooved, tubular pasta, penne's slender shape is perfect with tomato and cream sauces.

Capellini

Spaghettini

Spaghetti

Linguine

Fettuccine

Recipe Index (*Alphabetical*)

Recipe Index *(Alphabetical, cont.)*

Recipe Index *(Category)*

Recipe Index *(Category cont.)*

Recipe Index (*Italian*)